GW00374964

MORE EVERYDAY SAYINGS & THE BIBLE

Alan McIlwaine

Memory Lane
Productions

© Alan McIlwaine 2016

ISBN 978-1-909751-61-3

All scripture quotations are from
The New Scofield Reference Bible
(Authorised King James Version)
unless otherwise stated

Bold text, *italics*, brackets ( ) [ ] and
under-scoring have been added by the author to
emphasize selected words and,
where appropriate, clarify the context.

All extracts of Bible footnotes are
reproduced by permission.

Extracts from the Authorised Version of the Bible
(The King James Bible), the rights in which are vested
in the Crown, are reproduced by permission of the

Crown's Patentee, Cambridge University Press

Cover design: *Gary McIlwaine*

Memory Lane Productions

Email: everydaysayings@btinternet.com

Printed by J.C. Print Ltd., Belfast

This book is dedicated to my grandchildren:
Poppy, Heather, Eliza, Marianne,
Esther, James,
and George.

CONTENTS

Introduction

Everyday Saying

Page

1	Put words in my mouth	1
2	Root out!	3
3	Good for nothing!	5
4	A leopard cannot change its spots!	7
5	Am I my brother's keeper?	9
6	It never (even) crossed my mind!	11
7	There is nothing new under the sun	13
8	Grope in the dark	15
9	Hold my tongue / Hold your tongue	17
10	Take by the throat	19
11	A hair's breadth	21
12	A prophet is not without honour except in his own country	22
13	A (lone) voice in the wilderness	24
14	A heavy heart	26
15	A rose among thorns / between thorns	28
16	Spare the rod and spoil the child	30
17	A waster!	32
18	Fall out / Fell out	34
19	The fly in the ointment	37
20	Hoping against hope	39
21	Razed to the ground!	41
22	Turned the world upside down!	44
23	Make short work of it!	47
24	A stumbling stone / block	50
25	Clean gone!	52
26	Seeing is believing	55
27	More than enough	58
28	Little by little	60
29	To tell you the truth	62
30	The gospel truth	64

31 Sour grapes   66
32 Took him/her/them by the hand   69
33 The apple of my eye   72
34 In the land of the living   74
35 Wits' end!   77
36 Pride comes/goes before a fall   79
37 Right-hand man   83
38 See eye to eye   88
39 Two-edged sword / double edged sword   91
40 Cut to the heart!   94
41 Well able   97
42 A soft answer turneth away wrath   99
43 A word in season   101
44 The sun shines on the righteous   104
45 Set your (own) house in order   107
46 A red sky at night is a shepherd's delight; a red sky in the   111
    morning is a shepherd's warning!
47 Sign(s) of the times   114
48 It's not the end of the word!   117
49 In the twinkling of an eye   119
50 No rest for the wicked   122

Appendices

Appendix I   An adapted version of the hymn, *Count your blessings*
Appendix II   Acts 2:1-47
Appendix III   Acts 5:12-42
Appendix IV   Acts 6:1-7:60
Appendix V   List of Everyday Sayings covered in the first book

Introduction

Welcome to this companion volume of *More Everyday Sayings & The Bible!*

When reviewing the first volume [Everyday Sayings & The Bible] 15 years ago a well-known journalist commented that there were a lot more sayings in the Bible that deserved the same type of treatment! That comment startled me because I was not then aware of there being all that many beyond the fifty which comprised that book! How wrong I was!

As a matter of routine, but with no intention of writing a second book, I continued to bookmark all new sayings that I came across in the intervening years. However, the sheer number of my discoveries, and the repetitive use of them, has changed all that. The number of times that I have heard these sayings since putting pen to paper (or more accurately, starting to type) has confirmed to me that this new book is of God's will.

Another major factor in getting this companion volume to print was the number of favourable comments I received from persons all around the world in response to the first book. Many pointed out their favourite saying or sayings. Coupled with this was the number of requests seeking permission to use it in a variety of forums. This was humbling. However, no such permission is required. Those who find this volume useful are encouraged to make maximum use of it.

Getting any volume to print requires a lot of proofing, so, a special word of thanks to Helen and Jennifer who assisted to that end.

Researching this new volume has been a rich blessing to me. I have learned so much. My prayer is that all who read it will be similarly blessed.

Alan McIlwaine

Chapter 1

Put words in my mouth

One dictionary defines the expression as: *to interpret what someone said so that the words mean what you want and not what the speaker wanted.*

To hear the expression on the radio is one thing, but to hear it on the very day on which you intend to write about it is quite remarkable!

The expression (or the basis for it) is found at least seven times in the Bible – Exodus 4:15; Deuteronomy 18:18; 2 Samuel 14:3; 14:19; Isaiah 51:16; Isaiah 59:21 and Jeremiah 1:9. Interestingly enough, on all occasions it has a different meaning from that with which we generally associate it today.

In my experience it is only used in an interview or debate situation and then, only as a rebuke! And that was exactly the situation in today's radio interview when a political party leader used it. In true journalistic style the interviewer suggested what the interviewee's position might be in regard to a certain matter. Up to that point the interviewee had said absolutely nothing about it and, in retorting with our phrase, showed that he did not approve of the suggestion!

As already stated, all this is in contrast to the biblical scenarios of its use. For the sake of brevity we will focus only on the first and last of the references listed above. The background to their use is quite similar. God was calling two men to do a job: Moses (in the burning bush experience) to lead the Israelites out of Egypt and, many years later, Jeremiah to warn errant Judah of impending doom unless they turned from their sinful ways. Both men had reservations about their ability to speak for the Lord God but in each case He declared that He would enable them for the task by putting words in their mouth. With these assurances both men set about their tasks. (Jeremiah features again in our next saying.)

The two verses in question read —

*And thou shalt speak unto him, and **put words in his mouth**: and I will be with thy mouth, and with his mouth, and will teach you what ye shall do.* (Exodus 4:15)

*Then the LORD put forth his hand, and touched my mouth. And the LORD said unto me, Behold, I have **put my words in thy mouth**.* (Jeremiah 1:9)

Neither the expression under discussion nor, indeed, two of the key words in it ('words' and 'mouth') are used in a similar situation in the New Testament. The Lord Jesus had been warning His disciples of tough times ahead when they could be arrested and brought before the authorities because of their witness for Him. Nevertheless, He had a word of encouragement for them and we conclude by letting the verses speak for themselves — *And when they bring you unto the synagogues, and unto magistrates, and powers, take ye no thought how or what thing ye shall answer, or what ye shall say: For the Holy Ghost shall teach you in the same hour what ye ought to say.* (Luke 12:11-12)

Incidentally, the latter verse is not a licence for public speakers to engage in such addresses without first giving adequate time to preparation!

Chapter 2

Root out!

As with the previous saying, this too (along with another), was quoted by a different political party leader in a recent election debate. And some days later it was used three times in as many minutes on the BBC's Question Time programme when dealing with the subject of anti-Semitism. But what does the phrase 'root out' mean?

This exact phrase 'root out' is found three times in the AV of the Bible, namely Job 31:12, Isaiah 53:2 and Jeremiah 1:10. The middle one of these, which concerns the promised Messiah, has an entirely different meaning and will not be discussed just now.

There are other verses such as 1 Kings 14:15 where additional words are interposed between the two words of our saying, but still conveying the same meaning. And there may yet be others which do not contain the phrase, or either of the two words, but, nevertheless, express the same meaning.

Jeremiah got a brief mention in our previous chapter so let's see what the verse (1:10) of that prophecy says. Incidentally, it is the verse immediately following one of those containing our previous saying —

*See, I have this day set thee over the nations and over the kingdoms, to **root out,** and to pull down, and to destroy, and to throw down, to build, and to plant.*

The seven words immediately following the 'root out' phrase in the verse quoted clearly signify what the phrase means. However, one dictionary not only defines the phrase but goes a step further by suggesting a reason for the rooting out — *destroy completely, as if down to the roots (root out corruption) eradicate, exterminate, extirpate, uproot, defeat, smash to ribbons.* Thus, it is clear that it is used in circumstances where a bad situation exists and needs rectifying, and that is exactly the biblical context of its use as the few remaining verses of the chapter also make clear.

Jeremiah, like us today, lived in an age of idolatry and great sin. He was called upon by God to entreat the southern state of Judah to change her ways of living and to warn her of the consequences of failing to do so. As with today, most of Jeremiah's warnings fell on deaf ears. He then dictated his twenty years of labour to a scribe so that they could be read to temple-goers. When the then king learned of it he listened to a few of the scrolls' messages before cutting them up with a penknife and casting them into the fire.

The story does not end there but that will suffice for the moment. Some might well ask, "Is history on the verge of repeating itself?"

Chapter 3

Good for nothing!

We return to the book of Jeremiah for the first mention of this phrase, and then to the New Testament for the only other mention of it.

In our very first saying we learned what Jeremiah's mission and warning to Judah was all about. As time went by God used symbolism to reveal and reinforce things to Jeremiah. And it did not stop there. God later instructed Jeremiah on a number of occasions in the art of using symbolism against his target audiences to help get his message across. Indeed, the Lord Jesus used parables during His public ministry in a similar way.

Jeremiah's experiences included the remoulding of the marred vessel in the hands of the potter (Ch 18) and the smashing of the hardened earthen flask (Ch 19). However, we return to chapter 13 where God used symbolism to teach Jeremiah a certain truth.

Jeremiah was told to take a girdle (sash) and wear it. He was then told to hide it in a rock and return some time later to retrieve it. He did that only to find that the girdle had become marred and, not only was it not fit for purpose, it was of no use for anything! Using that illustration in 13:10 God made an analogy with rebellious Judah. The verse in question reads —

*This evil people, which refuse to hear my words, which walk in the imagination of their heart, and walk after other gods, to serve them, and to worship them, shall even be as this girdle, which is **good for nothing**.*

The verse is actually saying that God's chosen earthly people, like the girdle of the priestly garments, should have been holy, but in their sinful and rebellious ways brought no glory to Him at that time. Thus, they would be set aside and hence, good for nothing!

Our phrase, with the same teaching, was used by the Lord Jesus in the Sermon on the Mount. Matthew 5:13 reads —

*Ye are the salt of the earth: but if the salt has lost his savour, wherewith shall it be salted? It is thenceforth **good for nothing**, but to be cast out, and to be trodden under foot of men.*

Nothing more need be said here about the verse since this has already been commented upon in my previously published book under the saying, *The salt of the earth*.

Most will know that the phrase 'good for nothing' is just as often used to describe a human being as it is an inanimate object! In this connection it might interest you to know that years ago I knew someone who, in writing, was described as being useless. This brought a rebuke from senior management who declared, "Surely there is some good in every person." Food for thought!

Chapter 4

A leopard cannot change its spots!

A variant of this expression is *a leopard does not change its spots*.

The meaning of these expressions is that a person's character, especially if bad, will not change, even if they pretend it has. As one would expect, this is in keeping with the sentiments of Jeremiah 13:23, the only verse in the Bible that contains the basis for our saying —

> **Can the Ethiopian change his skin or the leopard his spots?**
> *Then may ye also do good, that are accustomed to do evil.*

Actually, there is a synonymous parallelism in the first part of the verse, but it is only the phrase about the leopard and his spots that has developed into an everyday saying. Perhaps political correctness has been in existence much earlier than we think!

Without going too much into the background, the northern kingdom of Israel had been taken over by Babylon whom Judah subsequently, and to their cost, foolishly regarded as being their ally. God, through Jeremiah, implored Judah to learn from Israel's mistake of abandoning Him and to stop flirting with Babylon, or otherwise face the consequences.

However, Judah had become hardened in her ways and what she was now doing had become 'natural' to her. To change this nature was just as difficult as it was for a black man (or a white man) to change the colour of their skin, or a leopard its spots. The context is implying the difficulty, rather than the impossibility that Judah would have in changing her ways, otherwise there was no point in Jeremiah giving repeated warnings. Judah's change involved morality while the Ethiopian's skin and the leopard's spots were a God-given nature.

Others might have a different understanding of the biblical use of this expression. However, two things are certain: leaving the biblical context aside, most people will agree on what we understand the expression to mean today, and that it is generally used in circumstances where there is skepticism about any genuine change in a situation/character.

Chapter 5

Am I my brother's keeper?

There are a number of interesting facts surrounding this saying which is found in the early chapters of Genesis.

The story is well known. Adam and Eve had been expelled from the Garden of Eden, Cain and Abel were born, sacrifices were offered with Cain's (fruit of the ground, non-blood) being rejected by God, but Abel's (firstling of his flocks, blood sacrifice) being accepted. Envy set in and Cain subsequently killed Abel. It is then that the verse containing our saying comes into play —

*And the Lord said unto Cain, Where is Abel thy brother? And he said, I know not: **Am I my brother's keeper?*** (Genesis 4:9)

God, being omniscient, knew what Cain did but in order to convict him of his foul deed asked the question. Cain's answer was partly a lie and, unknown to him, partly truth. The latter element is at the centre of our saying.

Not only did Cain answer the question but there is a sense in which he *answered it by asking another. The Lord Jesus did the same in circumstances that warranted it, but without deceit, unlike Cain who included a deliberate lie in his reply! Actually, the question that Cain asked was more of a statement and was tantamount to him saying that he was not his brother's keeper.

In the absence of some edict to the contrary, each person is responsible for themselves and their actions. Morally speaking, however, all mankind has an obligation to be mindful of the needs of others and, within reason, provide for them in a variety of ways. The aims of some charities are good examples of this.

In Cain's case his 'brother' was a sibling (blood brother)

although the meaning can be applied much wider. The same thought is illustrated by the parable of the Good Samaritan in answer to the question, 'Who is my neighbour?' in Luke chapter 10.

We have already indicated mankind's duty toward others and the limitations thereof. All too often, however, people try to control the lives of others and the result is nothing short of disaster. On the positive side, however, the Bible has lots of instruction for Christians in this regard and for your consideration here is a sample of the many verses —

Brethren, if a man be overtaken in a fault, ye which are spiritual, restore such an one in the spirit of meekness; considering thyself, lest thou also be tempted. (Galatians 6:1)

But ye, brethren, be not weary in well doing. And if any man obey not our word by this epistle, note that man, and have no company with him, that he may be ashamed. Yet count him not as an enemy, but admonish him as a brother. (2 Thessalonians 3:13-15)

If a brother or sister be naked, and destitute of daily food, And one of you say unto them, Depart in peace, be ye warmed and filled; notwithstanding ye give them not those things which are needful to the body; what doth it profit? (James 2:15-16)

And beside this, giving all diligence, add to your faith... and to brotherly kindness charity. (2 Peter 1:5, 7)

But whoso hath this world's good, and seeth his brother have need, and shutteth up his bowels of compassion from him, how dwelleth the love of God in him? (1 John 3:17)

*Just as a touch of humour, someone was once introduced to a Fermanagh man. "Oh", remarked the person being introduced, "are you one of those people who answer a question by asking another one?" "Who told you that?" came the reply!

Chapter 6

It never (even) crossed my mind!

A variant of this expression is, *it never (even) entered my head!*

It is generally in our denial of something, or in our defense of a possible shortcoming or missed opportunity, that we use this phrase to say that we didn't (even) think of it! It is entirely different from that of forgetfulness.

In an earlier chapter dealing with another saying *(Good for nothing)* we mentioned how that in the book of Jeremiah (and elsewhere) God often used symbolism to illustrate or reinforce something. Sometimes we call these things visual aids. We now arrive at two of the illustrations listed.

Firstly, in Jeremiah 18 we have the account of the marred clay being re-worked in the hands of the potter. The illustration was for the personal benefit of Jeremiah. On that occasion he was only a spectator. However, in chapter 19 he was to re-visit the potter's house but, this time, as a customer! He was to obtain a finished product in the shape of an earthen flask. It would be a symbol in at least two ways: speak of Judah in their hardened state, and secondly, show how it would be smashed to pieces unless their sinful practices changed. There then followed instructions as to his message and the smashing of the flask. It is implied by verse 14 that Jeremiah did as instructed and the chapter that follows details something of his subsequent persecution.

We go back to Jeremiah chapter 19 to get the background to his message in the smashing of the flask. One of the verses (v.5) contains the source of our saying —

*They have built also the high places of Baal, to burn their sons with fire for burnt offerings unto Baal, which I commanded not, nor spake it, **neither came it into my mind.***

There is a vast difference between saying something and commanding it, hence the inclusion of both phrases ('nor spake it' and 'I commanded not') in the verse! But why did God deem it necessary to include the closing phrase?

The expression is also found in Jeremiah 32:35 where it has the same meaning. A similar expression *neither came it into my heart*, found in Jeremiah 7:31 obviously has the same meaning. However, in Jeremiah 44:21 the words are re-arranged in the form of a question – *and came it not into his mind?* Thus, it is clear that the matter came to God's attention and would not be forgotten about. Punishment was inevitable!

God abhorred Judah's idolatry. At no stage did He ever command the building of an altar unto Baal or the offering of human sacrifices. In fact, He forbade it. Approximately 1,000 years earlier He gave Ten Commandments to Moses on Mount Sinai, the first three of which specifically commanded that they should have no other gods in preference to Him; should not make carved images; and should not bow down to them! Moreover, and crucial to our saying, the very thought of such corrupt practices never came to, entered, or crossed God's mind. How could it?

Looking ahead to the Millennium and the absence of the ark of the covenant, the expression also appears in Jeremiah 3:16 although there it has the connotation of no need or reason to remember it since God, in the Person of the Lord Jesus, will be in their midst!

Chapter 7

There is nothing new under the sun

Every time I ask a certain friend, "What's new?" one of us usually finish up quoting this proverb!

Everything I would like to say about it, and more, is covered on the gotquestions.org website which I reproduce here with their kind permission. They claim, rightly, that it is a common proverb and thus support my use of the 'everyday saying' terminology. Also, they are bold enough to state that the Bible is the origin! The article follows *Got Questions* customary question and answer format.

Question: "What does it mean that there is nothing new under the sun?"

Answer: Ecclesiastes 1:9 is the origin of what has become a common proverb, "There's nothing new under the sun." The verse reads like this: "What has been will be again, / what has been done will be done again; / there is nothing new under the sun." As a modern idiom, "there's nothing new under the sun" is often used as a world-weary complaint against life's monotony. When Solomon wrote the statement, he was emphasising the cyclic nature of human life on earth and the emptiness of living only for the "rat race."

The phrase "under the sun" is used 29 times in Ecclesiastes and nowhere else in Scripture. The intended meaning in Ecclesiastes is that what happens "under the sun" in a life separated from God is universal — the point of view in Ecclesiastes is an earth-bound perspective.

To say there is nothing new under the sun means there is nothing really new on the earth. All the activity of a man during his lifetime is lost in the grander scheme of things and will soon be forgotten (Ecclesiastes 1:11).

To say there is nothing new under the sun does not ignore inventions or advances in technology; rather, these innovations do not amount to any basic change in the world. In Solomon's time, many advances took place in society, but, from the larger perspective of life, human nature has remained and always will remain the same. The context of Ecclesiastes 1 discusses how the earth operates. The sun (verse 5), wind (verse 6), and water (verse 7) continue to function as they have in the past. Despite human efforts (verse 2), the world continues unchanged. Part of the writer's frustration from this observation is that "no one remembers the former generations, / and even those yet to come / will not be remembered / by those who follow them"(verse 11). People tend to forget the past, repeating its mistakes as a result.

Does the fact that there is nothing new under the sun mean that people should not try to improve themselves, the lives of others, or the world around them? The entire book of Ecclesiastes should be read before jumping to any conclusion. In the end, Solomon writes this: "Now all has been heard; / here is the conclusion of the matter: / Fear God and keep his commandments, / for this is the duty of all mankind. / For God will bring every deed into judgment, / including every hidden thing, / whether it is good or evil" (Ecclesiastes 12:13–14).

In other words, life involves more than what happens "under the sun." Living for God and His glory is the goal of life. Those who do not seek this goal will be judged. Even our good deeds that have gone unnoticed in this life are seen by God and will be rewarded in the future. This knowledge should result in a life lived for God, with a deep love for others and desire to make a difference.

Jeremiah 29:11 says, "'For I know the plans I have for you,' declares the LORD, 'plans to prosper you and not to harm you, plans to give you hope and a future.'" The Great Commission also gives a specific mission for the Christian life: "Go and make disciples of all nations, baptising them in the name of the Father and of the Son and of the Holy Spirit, and teaching them to obey everything I have commanded you" (Matthew 28:19–20). The Christian life is not meaningless. There may be nothing new under the sun, but Jesus promises, some day, to make all things new (Revelation 21:5).

Source: *"What does it mean there is nothing new under the sun?"*
Got Questions Ministries, n.d. Web. [26 May 2016]

Chapter 8

Grope in the dark

In my first book I dealt with ten everyday sayings from the book of Job and gave an overview of the book at pages 39-41. In chapters 2, 8, 9 and 34 of this book we deal with another four sayings.

Briefly, the book of Job consists of *a prologue* (Chs 1-2), *a dialogue* (Chs 3:1 - 42:6) and *an epilogue* (Ch 42:7-17). It is the dialogue section which contains the source of our four new sayings. The section contains three rounds of debate between Job and his three friends or, if you like, his so-called comforters! They came under the guise of sympathisers and finished up sermonisers!

For the want of a better expression, Job 'saw them coming'! He sat them out for a full week without a word being said. Then it started! Eliphaz was first to attack, then Bildad and finally, Zophar. Job answered each in turn. And, as if this wasn't bad enough, it was followed up with two more rounds and a spiel from Elihu on top of all that. They got Job's situation all wrong. If there is a lesson to be learned here it is that you are best to keep quiet unless you are qualified to give proper counsel, and in-depth at that!

Zophar, the last of the three to speak, is what we would call 'a know all'. He made wild statements and Job retorted. Job pointed out that he (Job) knew as much as him and his two friends, if not more! Among other things, he bore testimony to the wisdom and might of God. (Of course, this was only one side of the coin so to speak, but that is beyond our studies here.)

Halfway through his reply Job uses the phrase *grope in the dark* —

*They **grope in the dark** without light, and he maketh them to stagger like a drunken man.* (Job 12:25)

The substance of the phrase can be found in the following three references, but since Job is widely believed to be the first book of the Bible to be written it is obvious he is not quoting from these. The converse is likely to be the case. Of course, there may also have been other documents containing the phrase.

Deuteronomy 28:29
And thou shalt grope at noonday, as the blind gropeth in darkness, and thou shalt not prosper in thy ways: and thou shalt be only oppressed and spoiled evermore, and no man shall save thee.

Job 5:14
They meet with darkness in the daytime, and grope in the noonday as in the night.

Isa 59:10
We grope for the wall like the blind, and we grope as if we had no eyes: we stumble at noonday as in the night; we are in desolate places as dead men.

Job, in 12:25 is obviously speaking of the nations and their leaders. No doubt he used the phrase metaphorically. We all know what is to grope in the dark, literally.

One dictionary in trying to define the phrase states: *you grope for something, for example the solution to a problem, you try to think of it, when you have no real idea what it could be.*

As already indicated, there is more about Job and his sayings in the next chapter.

Chapter 9

Hold my tongue / Hold your tongue

This expression, although also mentioned earlier on by Job, comes hot on the heels of that covered in our previous chapter. It is found only twice in the Bible. Applying it to himself, Job used it on both occasions. Today it is mostly used as a command by one person to another viz., *hold your tongue.*

As children, *hold your tongue* was often on the lips of my mother. Mischievously, we sometimes responded by literally catching our tongue with finger and thumb! Of course, as already hinted, the phrase is used metaphorically.

As an aside, it is interesting to note how the tongue forms part of many of today's idioms, e.g., *on the tip of your tongue, tongue in cheek, speak with a forked tongue, a slip of the tongue, tongue-tied etc.*

Hold your tongue means to keep silent or refrain from speaking. 'Bite your tongue' is different in that it is the resisting of the urge to say something that you would otherwise say but for the time and place! 'Mum's the word' is different again; it has a secretive dimension. I suspect that the *hold your tongue* expression may be improperly used on other occasions but, rather than muddying the waters, I shall hold my tongue just now!

The two verses containing our phrase are —

Job 6:24
*Teach me, and I will **hold my tongue**: and cause me to understand wherein I have erred.*

Job 13:19
*Who is he that will plead with me? for now, if I **hold my tongue**, I shall give up the ghost.*

17

The context of use in these two verses is different. Eliphaz opens with the suggestion that there must be sin in Job's life because the innocent do not suffer (4:7). Wrong! Sin brings suffering, but not all suffering is the result of sin. In his reply Job uses our phrase for the first time. Unlike his second use of it, he is not saying, 'well, you show me where I went wrong and I will gladly stop complaining.' He is saying that he will give Eliphaz an opportunity to fully explain where he thinks he has gone wrong <u>without interrupting him</u>, but not necessarily accepting the explanation he gives.

As indicated, the second use of the phrase is different. Job uses it when rebuking Zophar, who completed Round 1 of the onset against him. In effect he is saying, 'convince me that I am wrong and I will not say another word.'

A little more of the structure of the debate is contained in our previous chapter.

Three things are worth noting in conclusion: (1) Job was perfect, upright, feared God, shunned evil and, not only was he greatest of all men of the east, God goes a stage further by stating that there was none like him in the earth!; (2) since the book of Job is generally regarded as being the earliest of all Bible writings it in effect means that he had no Scriptures to turn to for counsel; (3) during a most distressed state Job wished (a) that he had died at birth; (b) had never been born; (c) not even conceived; and (d) on a number of occasions wished that God would take life from him. Job asking God to take life from him is vastly different from him taking his own life! (What Job's wife meant in 2:9 by saying, 'Curse God and die' is beyond the scope of our studies here.)

Chapter 10

Take by the throat

The sole verse in the Bible containing this phrase is Matt.18:28 —

*But the same servant went out, and found one of his fellow-servants, which owed him an hundred pence: and he laid hands on him, and **took him by the throat**, saying, Pay me that thou owest.*

The word 'him' in our phrase is not in the original.

As with any verse of Scripture, it is generally best understood by examining the context. The latter half of chapter 18, although touching on forgiveness, is not the full doctrine on the subject. For instance, Luke 17:3-4 has something extra to say about it. Peter, in Matthew 18 only queries the number of times he should forgive someone and makes no reference to that person's admission or repentance of it, whereas in Luke 17 the Lord Jesus clearly taught the prerequisite of repentance.

Too many people today confuse the principle of forgiveness with that of not bearing malice or ill-will against people as taught in the Sermon on the Mount (Matthew 5). More information on this subject can be found in my tri-fold leaflet *Forgiveness — Full, Partial, Conditional or Unconditional?*

In Matthew 18 the Lord Jesus illustrates forgiveness by relating the parable of the King and his servants; in particular one who owed him a lot of money but who was not in a position to pay. He then pronounces judgment on the forgiven one who subsequently, in similar circumstances, failed to also show forgiveness. It was during his demands upon his fellow-servant that he physically *took him by the throat!*

Taking someone by the throat is to seize control. It is not unlike, but stronger than the idioms of *taking someone by the scruff of the neck*, or *taking the bull by its horns*. Typically, it is used by combatants in an attempt to handle or throttle their antagonists.

There are many instances of violence today when people are physically taken by the throat and threatened or pressurised into doing, or not doing, something. Quite often this involves the grabbing of someone by the two lapels and applying physical force of varying degrees and/or the issuing of a threat. But the idiom is also used in a metaphorical sense.

A good example of the intents behind the phrase, without it actually being quoted, is that of Nehemiah. Read chapter 13 of his book to see four problems he encountered in the rebuilding of the temple, and how he dealt with them head on. (Now, there's another saying!)

Chapter 11

A hair's breadth

Not only is our expression short, and it's meaning *the smallest possible distance, amount or degree*, but my comments are brief too!

The phrase is found only in Judges 20:16 —

*Among all this people there were seven hundred chosen men left- handed; every one could sling stones at **an hair breadth, and not miss**.*

The word 'breadth' is not in the original. However, the mere fact it is included in the widely read King James version justifies a mention here.

In a word, the phrase describes the accuracy of the warriors when hurling stones from a sling. They were very skilled. Today we call them marksmen or sharpshooters.

Did you notice that the seven hundred men were all left-handers? Interestingly, in 1 Chronicles 12:1-2 some among David's mighty men were both right and left-handed, thus skilled in another way. They were what we call, ambidextrous. Some current-day snooker players are that. As a painter and decorator I know how useful it would be to be able to paint with either hand!

A synonym of a hairs breadth is the expression *by the skin of one's teeth*. That saying is covered in pages 39-41 of my first book.

Chapter 12

A prophet is not without honour except in his own country

This saying is based on the words of the Lord Jesus who was Himself the greatest prophet of all —

*And they were offended in him. But Jesus said unto them, **A prophet is not without honour, save in his own country**, and in his own house. (*Matthew 13:57)

*But Jesus said unto them, **A prophet is not without honour, but in his own country**, and among his own kin, and in his own house.* (Mark 6:4)

It was only spoken once but is recorded by two different gospel writers. We choose Matthew's account for further explanation.

Midway through Matthew's gospel sees a crisis point. The nation of Israel had longed for a king that would smash the power of Rome and see them become an empire in their own right with all the benefits that would follow. However, their interests were purely political; one without any religious connotation in the sense of repentance of sin and wholehearted submission to the Saviour that had come.

In chapter 11 something of John the Baptist's preaching and imprisonment are recounted, and in chapter 12 Jesus was accused of working hand-in-hand with Satan and performing miracles under his power. Up until that point the nation had resisted their would-be King, but now with their blasphemous attack they had (informally) rejected Him. (Their official rejection was at Calvary!) Then, and not until then, does the

Lord Jesus in chapter 13 deliver the first six of the kingdom parables; the first three to the multitudes (including the disciples), and the last three privately to his disciples. (There are eight parables in all in the chapter but the first and last are not kingdom parables!)

The Lord Jesus then returns to His homeland of Nazareth and teaches in the synagogue. His fellow-countrymen knew exactly who He was, who His parents, brothers and sisters were, what His occupation in His pre public ministry days was, and were certain as to His unparalleled words and works. However, to use another idiom, familiarity breeds contempt, and in keeping with the then accepted attitude, they rejected Him. It was at that point the Lord Jesus used the expression that we are now studying. Consequently, and because of their unbelief, the Lord Jesus did very few miracles there.

Today, the expression is used of anyone whose talents and accomplishments are highly regarded by everyone except those of the person's homeland or those who are more familiar with the person.

Chapter 13

A (lone) voice in the wilderness

One dictionary defines this as: *someone who expresses an idea or opinion that is not popular.*

As inferred from the definition, the unpopularity of the idea or opinion holds the key; hence it is often a lone voice.

The expression's origin centres on John the Baptist, the forerunner of Jesus Christ. He was called the Baptist, not because of his acts of baptism — which he did — but because of the doctrine of baptism which formed part of his message. However, he was a prophet – one whose coming was foretold some 700 years earlier by the prophet Isaiah. Part of that prophecy contains the expression —

The voice of him that crieth in the wilderness, Prepare ye the way of the Lord. (Isaiah 40:3)

Another prophet, Malachi, although not mentioning the phrase under study, also speaks of John's future coming.

The opening chapters of all four Gospel accounts make reference to John the Baptist (and Isaiah's prophecy concerning him), and similarly contain the expression —

Matthew 3:3
*For this is he that was spoken of by the prophet Esaias, saying, **The voice of one crying in the wilderness**, Prepare ye the way of the Lord, make his paths straight.*

Mark 1:3
***The voice of one crying in the wilderness**, Prepare ye the way of the Lord, make his paths straight.*

Luke 3:4
*As it is written in the book of the words of Esaias the prophet,
saying,* **The voice of one crying in the wilderness,** *Prepare
ye the way of the Lord, make his paths straight.*

John 1:23
He said, I am the voice of one crying in the wilderness, *Make
straight the way of the Lord, as said the prophet Esaias.*

In addition to the Scriptures referred to above, there are
further references to John the Baptist in Matthew 11:1-15;
Luke 7:19-35; Acts 13:14-43 and, concerning his murder,
Matthew 14:1-12 and Mark 6:14-29. It is interesting to note
that John's murder is not recorded contemporaneously in the
same way as Stephen's, but, rather, retrospectively.

Much could be said about John the Baptist – his garments
were different from that of the priests, his diet was different and, of
course, so, too, was his message. Speaking of John, the Lord Jesus
could say, *Among them that are born of women there hath not
risen a greater than John the Baptist.* (Matthew 11:11; Luke 7:28)

John, as forerunner, had the privilege of introducing the
Lord Jesus on the banks of the Jordan. Pointing to him, he
could say, *Behold the Lamb of God, who taketh away the sin
of the world.* (John 1:29) In contrast to the Lamb of God,
Old Testament sacrifices were made for a remembrance of sin,
and were limited to the nation of Israel.

As the son of a priest [Zechariah], John was entitled to the
priestly office and all the trappings that went with it. However,
God had already removed His presence from the Temple
because of His peoples' sins. So, disassociating himself from
all the warped trappings of the Temple John went into the
wilderness and proclaimed the coming of the Messiah from
there, hence the expression, *a (lone) voice in the wilderness.*

John the Baptist was certainly a lone voice but the use
of the word 'one' in the phrase, *the voice of one crying in the
wilderness,* is more likely to refer to him as being the appointed
one as opposed to the singularity of the number.

Chapter 14

A heavy heart

A heavy heart is one that has a feeling of sadness or unhappiness, or is weighed down by burdens.

The expression is found only in Proverbs 25:20 which reads —

*As he that taketh away a garment in cold weather, and as vinegar upon nitre, so is he that singeth songs to an **heavy heart**.*

Solomon wrote the book of Proverbs. Since he has been referred to briefly in chapter 7, and will be further mentioned in later chapters, it is appropriate to say something about him here. Solomon was the last king of the united kingdom of Israel before it was divided into the northern and southern kingdoms. He succeeded his father David who had succeeded Saul, the very first king. He built the first temple.

Solomon also wrote Ecclesiastes, the Song of Solomon and two of the Psalms (72 and 127). Proverbs is the middle one of the five poetical books (Job, Psalms, Proverbs, Ecclesiastes, and Song of Solomon).

The actual proverbs in what is known as the book of Proverbs do not start until chapter 10. Thereafter, they are divided into different sections. The section comprising chapters 25–29 (which contains our saying) was composed by Solomon but copied years later by the men of Hezekiah, king of Judah. His proverbs in that section total 140. We know from 1 Kings 4:32 that Solomon wrote (spoke) 3,000 in all, and a further 1,005 songs.

A lot of the proverbs have nothing in common other than principle. For example, the verse containing our saying is really in two parts and, as explained below, is of synthetic parallelism.

With so many pithy sayings in the book of Proverbs one would expect to find a deluge of everyday sayings, but there is only a handful, e.g., a double-edged sword, 5:4; spare the rod and spoil the child, 13:24; a soft answer turneth away wrath, 15:1; a word in season, 15:23; pride cometh/goeth before a fall, 16:18; a (great) waster, 18:9; a heavy heart, 25:20; we don't know what a day brings forth, 27:1. Not all everyday sayings are proverbs, nor are all proverbs everyday sayings!

The preceptaustin.org website is helpful with regard to the literary form of the proverbs (mostly couplets) written by Solomon. It states —

The two clauses of the couplet are generally related to each other by what has been termed parallelism, according to Hebrew poetry. Three kinds of parallelism have been pointed out:

1. Synonymous Parallelism. Here the second clause restates what is given in the first clause. Judgments are prepared for scorners / And stripes for the back of fools. Prov. 19:29

2. Antithetic Parallelism. Here a truth which is stated in the first clause is made stronger in the second clause by contrast with an opposite truth. The light of the righteous rejoiceth / But the lamp of the wicked shall be put out. Prov. 13:9

3. Synthetic Parallelism. The second clause develops the thought of the first. The terror of a king is as the roaring of a lion / He that provoketh him to anger sinneth against his own life. Prov. 20:2.

Returning specifically to our saying and the biblical context of its use, under normal circumstances one would think that singing to someone (unless you had a voice like mine!) would cheer them up. But the key here is the *heavy heart.* Unless the recipient is in the correct frame of mind it would be similar to rubbing salt into the wound!

Chapter 15

A rose among thorns / between two thorns

Although a well-known saying, my research reveals very little information about it. Again, the precise phrase is not found in the Bible but the basis for it most likely comes from two successive verses in the Song of Solomon.

As the complete title suggests, not only was the Song written by Solomon, but the opening words, 'The song of songs' would also suggest that he regarded it as his best song. As stated in our previous chapter, we know from 1 Kings 4:32 that Solomon wrote 1,005 songs.

Speaking of the Song, the beloved J Sidlow Baxter said —
'There is no book of Scripture on which more commentaries have been written and more diversities of opinion expressed than this short poem of eight chapters.'

The language of the Song is oriental and it is best read with that in mind. There are many similes in the Song such as *'like'* and *'as'* and a host of metaphors (figures of speech in which a word or phrase is applied to something that it does not literally denote in order to imply a resemblance).

In so many ways the Song is like a drama with a dialogue between at least five main sets of speakers namely, the Shulamite woman, Daughters of Jerusalem (friends of the Shulamite), the Shulamite's shepherd-lover, God, and the Shulamite's brothers. Unfortunately, some regard King Solomon and the shepherd-lover as the one and same person. The big problem, of course, is determining who the speaker is on a great many occasions.

Generally speaking, there are three differing views as to what the Song is all about. Some regard it as nothing more than a literal love story about the Shulamite women and her shepherd-lover. Others view it as allegorical in the sense that it speaks of God and the nation of Israel. Finally, the remainder, who also take the allegorical approach, apply it to Christ and His church (and individual members within it).

Commenting on the Song of Solomon, the great Bible teacher Warren W. Wiersbe, says, "While the Song of Solomon illustrates the deepening love we can have with Christ, we must be careful not to turn the story into an allegory and make everything mean something. All things are possible to those who allegorise, and what they come up with is usually heretical." Worth pondering!

We now come to our saying which is reflected in the words of Song of Solomon 2:1-2. The verses read —

*I am the **rose** of Sharon, and the lily of the valleys.* (v.1)
*As the lily **among thorns**, so is my love among the daughters.* (v.2)

I regard the Shulamite woman to be the speaker in verse 1, and her shepherd-lover the speaker in verse 2. (Some think it is Solomon.) Whoever the speaker may be has no effect on our saying. Metaphorically, he was comparing the beauty of the Shulamite with other women and this is still how the saying is used today.

Generally speaking, the phrase is used humorously. No real sincerity, especially a degradation of those who are the 'thorns', is intended. This is very much accepted, just as on those occasions when the phrase is used of a man sitting between two women! All is said in jest!

Everyone knows the contrast between roses and thorns; one is beautiful and soft, the other hard and prickly. However, I understand that the rose (of Sharon) in the verses referred to is not a rose as we know it today. It may be a flower more aligned to the lily mentioned in the same verse. We do not need to pursue that aspect here since any flower is an adequate contrast with thorns.

Finally, while generally (and jestingly) used in connection with beauty (looks), it can also be used to distinguish between the sexes, attributes, etc.

Chapter 16

Spare the rod and spoil the child

This is an increasingly controversial subject and I hazard to guess that few need any explanation as to what it means.

The actual phrase is not in the Bible. Some claim that it is from a 17th century poem by Samuel Butler. Regardless, the sentiments of the saying are in at least six verses of the Bible – all from the book of Proverbs. The verses read —

Proverbs 13:24
He that spareth his rod hateth his son: but he that loveth him chasteneth him betimes.

Proverbs 19:18
Chasten thy son while there is hope, and let not thy soul spare for his crying.

Proverbs 22:15
Foolishness *is bound in the heart of a child; but the rod of correction shall drive it far from him.*

Proverbs 23:13-14
Withhold not correction from the child: for if thou beatest him with the rod, he shall not die. Thou shalt beat him with the rod, and shalt deliver his soul from hell.

Proverbs 29:15
The rod and reproof give wisdom: but a child left to himself bringeth his mother to shame.

Much could be said about the tightening of laws in the last forty years banning capital and corporal punishment. It is not an area that

I need go into here other than to say that the degree of punishment involved in the categories mentioned is well beyond the levels envisaged in the verses just quoted.

It is scriptural to say that punishment must always fit the crime. For instance, take the maxim of 'an eye for an eye, and a tooth for a tooth' as found in Matthew 5:38. Many, unfortunately, interpret it as justification for revenge, when the true meaning is that the punishment should fit the crime; in other words, not excessive.

Criminologists have researched laboriously and scores of books have been written on these matters. However, the above verses are clear in their teaching. Incidentally, some believe that Solomon issued them on the basis of how he treated his son. That opens up another argument too great to be discussed here.

Two things on a personal level: over long years I have seen the varying methods of applying the rod principle. What is beyond dispute is the fact that wrongdoing must be dealt with, whatever form it may take. Secondly, I often got the rod, both at home and at school and, as the saying goes, it never did me a button of harm. (I can envisage my siblings and my offspring smiling at this point!)

All this brings us to the teaching of Hebrews 12 – '*Furthermore we have had fathers of our flesh which corrected us, and we gave them reverence (v.9) ....Now no chastening for the present seemeth to be joyous, but grievous: nevertheless afterward it yieldeth the peaceable fruit of righteousness unto them which are exercised thereby.*' (v.11)

Chapter 17

A waster!

There is a close affinity between this saying and *the good for nothing* saying in chapter 3.

A waster is simply someone, or something that wastes. For example a person could waste time or, alternatively, do nothing constructive with their life considering the opportunities afforded them. Also, the regular sowing of a moss killer on the lawn may be regarded by some as a money waster.

The word 'waster' is found twice in the Bible. In the first, Proverbs 18:9, it is combined with the adjective 'great', thus magnifying the effect. The verse likens the slothful (lazy) person to that of a great waster; they are both of a kind. The verse reads —

*He also that is slothful in his work is brother to him that is **a great waster**.* (Proverbs 18:9)

Sufficient has been said in chapter 14 about the book of Proverbs, its author and structure without the need to repeat it here.

The second occurrence of the word is in Isaiah 54:16 —

*Behold, I have created the smith that bloweth the coals in the fire, and that bringeth forth an instrument for his work; and I have created the **waster** to destroy.*

The teaching here is in connection with the oppression that God's people are under. God is reminding us of who is in control. Just as the maker of weapons of war are under His control, so, too, are they that use them for that purpose. Neither person can go further than what God permits. A good illustration of this is the limits to which God allowed

Satan to attack Job (Job chapters 1 and 2).

Truths like this are of great comfort to God's people of every generation and, in essence, are the things that keep them going.

Chapter 18

Fall out / Fell out

This term has various meanings. One is *to drop out* or *become detached;* others include *disagreement, argument, row, quarrel,* etc. It is on the latter ones we concentrate here. Incidentally, the phrase should not be confused with the compound 'fallout' which means *an adverse and unwanted secondary effect.*

The precise term 'fall out' is found only in Ezekiel 30:22, but it's meaning there is outside the scope of our study. However, it is, in essence, found in Genesis 45:24, with the interposition of the word 'not' into the phrase. The verse reads —

*So he sent his brethren away, and they departed: and he said unto them, See that ye **fall** not **out** by the way.* (Genesis 45:24)

This verse comes midway through the well known story of Joseph, a story loved by children and adults alike!

The intriguing story of Joseph is beautifully summarised in the gotquestions.org website under the question: "What should we learn from the life of Joseph?" With their permission I reproduce the relevant part of the posting —

Joseph was the 11th son of Jacob, and his story is found in Genesis 37–50. As a 17-year-old shepherd, Joseph is something of a tattle- tale, bringing a bad report about his brothers to their father (Genesis 37:2). This behaviour, combined with Jacob's overt favouritism towards Joseph, causes his older brothers to resent him to the point of hatred (37:3-4). Because of Jacob's open love for Joseph, his favouritism was begrudged by his other sons. And when Jacob presented Joseph with a highly decorated coat, he was hated and resented by his brothers all the more (Genesis 37:3). To make matters worse, Joseph begins relating his dreams — prophetic visions showing Joseph one day ruling over his family (Genesis 37:11-15). The animosity towards Joseph peaks when his brothers plot to kill him in the wilderness. Reuben, the eldest, objects to outright murder, so instead, the brothers sell Joseph as a slave and deceive their father into thinking his favourite son had been slain by wild beasts (Genesis 37:18-35).

Joseph is sold to a high-ranking Egyptian named Potiphar and eventually becomes the supervisor of Potiphar's household. In Genesis 39 we read of how Joseph excelled at his duties and became one of Potiphar's most trusted servants and was put in charge of his household. Potiphar could see that, whatever Joseph did, God looked favourably on him and he prospered in all that he did. However, Potiphar's wife attempts to seduce Joseph, and when her advances are rebuffed, she falsely accuses him of attempted rape. Joseph, although innocent in the matter, is cast into prison (Genesis 39:7-20). In jail, Joseph interprets the dreams of two of his fellow prisoners. Both interpretations prove to be true, and one of the men is later released from jail and restored to his position as the king's cupbearer (40:1-23). Two years later, the king himself has some troubling dreams, and the cupbearer remembers Joseph's gift of interpretation. The king calls for Joseph and relates his dreams. Joseph predicts seven years of bountiful harvests followed by seven years of severe famine in Egypt and advises the king to begin storing grain in preparation for the coming dearth (41:1-37). For his wisdom, Joseph is made a ruler in Egypt, second only to the king (41:38-49).

When the famine strikes, even Canaan is affected, and Jacob sends ten of his sons to Egypt to buy grain (Genesis 42:1-3). While there, they meet their long-lost brother, whom they do not recognise. Joseph's brothers bow down to him, fulfilling the earlier prophecy. Joseph then reveals his identity to his brothers and forgives their wrongdoing. Jacob and his family move to Egypt to be with Joseph. Jacob's descendants stay in Egypt for 400 years, until the time of Moses. When Moses leads the

Hebrews out of Egypt, he takes the remains of Joseph with him, as Joseph had requested (Genesis 50:24- 25; cf. Exodus 13:19).

Source: "What should we learn from the life of Joseph?" Got Questions Ministries, n.d. Web. [6 May 2016]

In addition to being familiar with the expression, it would be unusual if most of us have not been involved in some sort of a fall out at one time or another! Because of these propensities, one could be forgiven for thinking this was the reason for Joseph giving such a warning. But there are stronger reasons!

Joseph knew that on their way back home his brothers would be recalling the part that each of them played in the events that led to him being sold into Egypt, and that their wickedness would soon have to come to the knowledge of their father. Due to human nature, they would be prone to blaming each other (with the expected consequences) which is exactly what Rueben did a few chapters earlier during their first meeting with Joseph. That first indication of the blame game can be found in chapter 42 verses 7- 22. Please note the last two verses in particular.

In conclusion, two other verses come to mind – *Behold, how good and how pleasant it is for brethren to dwell together in unity!* (Psalm 133:1) and, *If it be possible, as much as lieth in you, live peaceably with all men.* (Romans 12:18)

Chapter 19

The fly in the ointment

This expression means: *a drawback, whether by a thing or person, which was not first apparent and spoils an otherwise enjoyable situation.* One might say, for example, "I like my new house but the fly in the ointment is that nosey neighbour who is always peeping over the hedge!"

The basis for the expression is found in Ecclesiastes 10:1 —

Dead flies cause the ointment of the apothecary to send forth a stinking savour: so doth a little folly him that is in reputation for wisdom and honour.

Some chapters earlier in this book we touched briefly on Solomon and how that he authored the last three books of the poetical section of the Old Testament – Proverbs, Ecclesiastes, and Song of Solomon. This is the order in which they appear although it is generally accepted that Solomon wrote the Song first (when younger), Proverbs next (in middle age) and Ecclesiastes last (later in life). We reminded ourselves of the fact that Solomon did not practice all that he preached!

Solomon's experiences (and disappointments) in life are the key to the book of Ecclesiastes. Many question if there is life after death but this was not Solomon's problem; he was more interested in experiencing real life before death! From a human point of view he tried to see the end of everything. He studied extensively and concluded that science, philosophy, pleasure, materialism, fatalism, deism, egotism, religion, wealth and morality did not provide the solution. In contrast, he declared, '*Fear God and keep His commandments; for this is the whole duty of man. For God shall bring every work into judgment, with every secret thing, whether it be good, or whether it be evil.'* (Ecclesiastes 12:13-14)

As an aside, such a declaration by Solomon would suggest that he may have recovered somewhat from his sinful manner of life. With that background we now come to our saying.

Some years ago a family member discovered a dead fly in their soup. It was off-putting. That part of the story ends there but the effect, however, was similar to that of a dead fly in ointment. Ointments smell good, dead flies do not. That is the literal aspect of the saying.

However, Solomon was using the statement metaphorically and as follow-on from the final comment in the previous chapter: *'...but one sinner destroyeth much good.'* The verse containing the basis for our saying (v.1) makes it clear that it was reputation which was at stake. Earlier in chapter 7 verse 1 Solomon could say, *'A good name is better than precious ointment...'* The lesson is simple; the smallest of things can do great damage. 1 Corinthians 5:6 states, *'a little leaven leaveneth the whole lump.'*

Chapter 20

Hoping against hope

This expression has been variously described as: *having hope even when the situation appears to be hopeless; hoping or wishing for (something) with little reason or justification.*

The expression, or more accurately the basis for it, is found in Romans 4:18. The verse reads —

Who against hope believed in hope, *that he might become the father of many nations, according to that which was spoken, so shall thy seed be.*

In order to understand the expression in the biblical context one needs to read verses 13-21.

Romans 3:21-5:21 deal with the subject of 'justification by faith'. Chapter 4 illustrates how this was seen in the Old Testament by using the examples of Abraham and David. The verse containing our saying is in the section dealing with Abraham which, incidentally, is only a summary. One needs to read Genesis chapters 5-18 to get a fuller account.

One would not deny that the first half of Romans chapter 4 is not the easiest understood, particularly in the Authorised Version. However, reading it a number of times helps to get a better understanding.

The latter half, which contains our saying, is straightforward and much of it is based on the full story of Abraham, his wife Sarah, and the promise of a child of their own. You can read about it in Genesis chapters 15-18, but in summary it concerns a man (almost 100 years old) who had a wife about 10 years his junior and well past childbearing age. Despite the generality of the situation, Abraham believed God who, twenty years earlier, promised that He would give them both a child of their own. Under normal circumstances they would have had little reason to believe that this was possible. Abraham had hope (faith) in what was otherwise a hopeless situation.

The word 'hope' appears 130 times in the Bible and is an interesting study in itself. However, if you are a young person or, indeed, not so young, and enjoy a good adventure story then why not read the last two chapters of Acts (27 & 28). They recount the Apostle Paul's voyage to Rome and the shipwreck towards the end. Discover how that the master of the ship and crew had given up all hope of survival. Discover also how Paul received an assurance from the angel of God that they would make it to Rome. In a sense, his hope was pitted against the hope (or lack of it) of the master of the ship and crew.

Still on the subject of hope, we close with a verse of a well known hymn —

> My hope is built on nothing less
> Than Jesus' blood and righteousness;
> I dare not trust the sweetest frame,
> But wholly lean on Jesus' name.
>
> *On Christ, the solid rock, I stand;*
> *All other ground is sinking sand,*
> *All other ground is sinking sand.*
>
> When darkness veils his lovely face,
> I rest on his unchanging grace;
> In every high and stormy gale,
> My anchor holds within the veil.
>
> His oath, his covenant, his blood
> Support me in the whelming flood;
> When all around my soul gives way,
> He then is all my hope and stay.
>
> When he shall come with trumpet
> sound, O may I then in him be found,
> Dressed in his righteousness alone,
> Faultless to stand before the throne.

Chapter 21

Razed to the ground!

This saying is based on Psalm 137:7. Since it is the first of a few sayings from the book of Psalms covered in this volume we take the opportunity to give something of their structure.

The Psalms are divided into five sections or books; the latter being Psalms 107-150 which contain the verse forming the basis of our saying. These final 44 Psalms are essentially Psalms of the Captivity and Return to Jerusalem. As with all the preceding Psalms and, as inferred from the section title ascribed, they are connected with God's earthly people Israel. That is not to say that New Testament believers cannot benefit from them; quite the contrary. (I cherish the poem, *Bible Books in Verse*, with the line on the Psalms which reads, *'And David's Psalms are precious to every child of God.'*)

A number of the Psalms, of which Psalm 137 is last, are known as imprecatory Psalms. These call upon God to deal with the oppressor in judgment. While it is true of Judah historically, it is equally true of the future end times when the godly remnant in the Great Tribulation will call upon God to overthrow the then oppressive Gentile world power. You can read more about this in Matthew chapter 24.

Warren Wiersbe, who has the art of summarising Bible chapters like no other, gives this comprehendible summary —

This psalm came out of Israel's exile in Babylon, and it can serve as an inventory of your spiritual life today.

What makes you weep (1)? The Jews wept as they remembered the past, but they did not weep over their sins. They wept because their sins caught up with them, not because they had sinned.

What makes you sing (2–4)? They lost their song, so they hung up their harps. David had a similar experience (Ps. 32:1–7). Can you sing praises to God in a difficult place (Acts 16:25)? Can you praise the Lord at all times?

What makes you yearn (5–6)? What is the ache in your heart? What do you long for more than anything else? Is it in God's will?

What makes you angry (7–9)? God had promised to judge Babylon (Isa. 13; note v. 16), so they were praying in His will; but the note of anguish is missing. (See the entry on Ps. 58 for comments on the "imprecatory psalms.") If you love the Lord, you must hate evil (Ps. 97:10; Rom. 12:9) but leave the judgment to the Lord (Rom. 12:17– 21).

Source: With the Word: The Chapter-by-Chapter Bible Handbook

Wiersbe's final comment above distinguishes between the attitude of God's earthly people and that advocated for His heavenly people, the church!

The Psalms, which are also known as Songs, are still sung in some congregations today. Indeed, Psalm 23 (to the tune of Amazing Grace) was one of my wedding hymns!) But, is it not remarkable that a substantial part of Psalm 137 features in the internationally known 'Rivers of Babylon' song of the 1970's which has been a top ten best-selling single in the UK? Perhaps the catchy tune played a large part! Those of that era will remember Mary McKee and the Genesis singing it. (I still play it today.) Is it not ironic, that despite the Psalm recalling sad circumstances in which anyone would find it difficult to sing, that the sentiments of the Psalm are now widely known through singing?

And now to our saying; some hearing it quoted have been confused. They, because of the same sounding word 'raised', have questioned how this could be (unless you are working underground!). The telltale is in their spelling of the word when quoting the phrase! Incidentally, some Bible translations spell the word with an 's' (rase). Actually, it is from the customary spelling that we get the word 'razor'.

The expression *razed to the ground* simply means *to demolish* or *lay flat* as in the destruction of a building or a city. That is the thought in Psalm 137 when the returned exiles recalled the words of the enemy in their desire to destroy their beloved Jerusalem. The verse containing the basis for our saying reads —

Remember, O Lord, the children of Edom in the day of Jerusalem; who said, **raze it, raze it, even to the foundation** *thereof.* (Psalm 137:7)

Chapter 22

Turned the world upside down!

This expression is found only once in the Bible. However, the shorter phrase, 'turned upside down' (or variants of it), which is an integral part of it, is found in 2 Kings 21:13, Psalm 146:9, Isaiah 24:1 and Isaiah 29:16. In its simplest form it means *inverted,* but in certain cases it can mean *topsy-turvy* which suggests *a state of disorder.* Such a meaning leads on nicely to our full expression and saying.

Suggested meanings of the full expression range from a *change to the status quo* to *disorientate.* These things often occur suddenly and can make one confused and/or extremely upset with an unwelcoming outcome. It has a more serious connotation than the expression 'upsetting the apple cart'.

Among other things the book of Acts, otherwise known as the Acts of the Apostles, record the three missionary journeys of the Apostle Paul viz., chapters 13-14; 15:36-18:22; and 18:23-21:14, respectively. It is in the chapters that deal with the second missionary journey that our expression occurs (17:6). Perhaps chapters 16 and 17 are among the better known chapters – chapter 16 for the 'Macedonian Call', the conversion of the first European (Lydia), the imprisonment of Paul and Silas/ conversion of the Philippian jailer, and chapter 17 for events concluding with Paul's famous sermon on Mars Hill.

Chapters 4 onward record many persecutions of the apostles and other early Christians. Some involved imprisonment. Paul (who at that stage was called Saul) was involved in this. Read chapter 7 for the account of Stephen's martyrdom. However, in chapter 9 Paul is converted on the Damascus Road and later commences his missionary journeys.

The same chapters, however, also record the conversion of many souls. Phrases such as 'many believed' are used repeatedly.

Evangelism was now on the move; even in such places as the Jewish synagogues which the opening verses of chapter 17 record.

While there were many that believed, there were also those that were hostile to the message. When efforts in Thessalonica to 'track down' Paul failed, they arrested those whom they thought were 'harbouring' him (v.7) and made the accusations in the verse (Acts 17:6) that contains our saying —

*And when they found them not, they drew Jason and certain brethren unto the rulers of the city, crying, These that have **turned the world upside down** are come hither also*;

The words 'contrary', 'another King' and 'troubled' in verses 7 and 8 go some way to show in what way their world was turned upside down. Here are the two verses in full —

Whom Jason hath received: and these all do contrary to the decrees of Caesar, saying that there is another king, one Jesus. And they troubled the people and the rulers of the city, when they heard these things.

The puritan commentator John Gill, who gets another mention later, makes the following comment —

'these that have turned the world upside down': the Syriac version reads, "the whole earth": the apostles, according to the cry of these men, had thrown the whole world into disorder, and had made disturbances in kingdoms and cities, wherever they came; and had made innovations in religion, and turned men from their old way of worship to another; and are come hither also; to make the like disorders and disturbances, as elsewhere.

We indicated much earlier that our saying is usually associated with unwelcome events. Let us finish with good news. The message of the gospel (which is good news) has the opposite effect. It can change lives for the better. It brings a new purpose to life, new hope, and a new destiny in eternity. Is it any wonder the apostle Paul could say in Romans 1:16 —

For I am not ashamed of the gospel of Christ: for it is the power of God unto salvation to everyone that believeth.

Chapter 23

Make short work of it!

Since this expression, and the one to follow, is found within a few verses of each other in Romans chapter 9, the one introduction will suffice. As with most other expressions, the context of use is all- important.

In a previous chapter of this book we made reference to the three missionary journeys of the apostle Paul as recorded in the book of Acts. The 3rd of those journeys is where we take up the story.

It was during this 3rd missionary journey that Paul visited Corinth, and it was from there that he wrote his epistle to the Romans (around AD 56). He intended visiting the believers in Rome and the epistle was an interim measure. Incidentally, his address was to the 'saints' there as opposed to the 'church' since the believers were likely gathering in small groups rather than a larger church as we know it today.

The book of Romans comprehensively covers the central themes of Christianity. Early on Paul talks about the 'gospel of God' (of which he was not ashamed). Then, amongst other things, he points out that all are sinners — Jew and Gentile alike — and proceeds to talk about great doctrines such as that of faith and justification.

At first sight Paul seems to go off on a tangent when he reaches chapters 9, 10 and 11. But this is not the case. Despite being born a Jew, upon conversion and the call of God Paul became the apostle to the Gentiles and, in their state of ignorance (lack of under-standing), this caused difficulties for the Roman believers. So, Paul, under the guidance of the Holy Spirit, took opportunity to set the record straight. This involved going back into history and, even further, into the eternal counsels of God.

While both matters involve election, it is important to

differentiate here between the election of Israel as a nation (God's earthly people) and individual members of the universal church of God, which are God's heavenly people. Failure to see this distinction is the cause of much confusion today.

Verses 4 and 5 are the keystone to all that follows in chapters 9-11. The two verses record eight things regarding the legitimacy of the Jewish faith. However, in the plan of God this faith system had its limitations. Gentiles were also to be brought into the good of things and both, through the sacrificial death of Christ at Calvary, would be reconciled to God.

As one reads on through chapter 9 they will see how Paul argues the case for both the sovereignty and faithfulness of God. Among other things, he sets out how Israel, despite their election, was temporarily set aside by God because of their sin. It was at that stage the Gentiles came into blessing. All this was in the eternal counsels of God and are not we, who were once Gentiles, glad!

Paul goes on to deal with the so-called absurdity of how the Jew, despite having the law 'lost out' to the Gentiles who theretofore had no desire after God. The difference was this; the Jew made self- efforts to obtain righteousness, whereas the Gentile obtained it by true faith in God. (Read more about this in connection with our next saying.)

However, Israel will feature again in the 'end times' plan of God. Paul's teaching in the chapter, by referring to a number of Old Testament prophecies, brings us to the verse (v.28) containing the expression which has now become an everyday saying. The verse reads —

*For he will finish the **work**, and cut it **short** in righteousness: because a short work will the Lord make upon the earth.*

It is interesting to note that the verse actually makes double reference to 'short work'. It is generally accepted that Paul here is quoting from Isaiah 10:23 and thus it is clear that the verse ultimately refers to the yet future events during the Great Tribulation in the end times. The emphasis is on the speed and finality with which God will deal with the then Gentile world power upon His return to earth. From a timing point of view, the phrase has a connection with another phrase "except those days should be shortened..." (Matthew 24:22) [More properly translated, *short* or as the HCSB translates it, *unless those days were limited,*] but, pardon the pun, that is the limit of the matter; the phrases have entirely different meanings!

The expression, as we use it today, likewise refers to the speed in which some particular thing is done. On occasions it can be applied to persons also and, sadly, in many instances death or serious injury results.

Returning to spiritual matters, we close by quoting Warren Wiersbe who said – "the emphasis in Romans 9 is on *Israel's past election*, in Romans 10 on *Israel's present rejection*, and in Romans 11 on *Israel's future restoration*. Israel is the only nation in the world with a complete history – past, present, and future."

Chapter 24

A stumbling stone / block

As stated in the previous chapter, this saying is found within a few verses of our last saying (and elsewhere). This enables us to keep our comments to an absolute minimum as regards the background of its use there.

We go back as far the Jews inability to understand how the Gentiles 'pipped them to the post' in regard to obtaining the righteousness of God. They thought that their religious pursuits, albeit tinged with self-effort, left them better qualified. As Paul explained, this was not the case and thus it became a big stumbling point for them.

After a comprehensive exposition Paul concludes his argument at the end of the chapter by stating —

What shall we say then? That the Gentiles, which followed not after righteousness, have attained to righteousness, even the righteousness which is of faith. But Israel, which followed after the law of righteousness, hath not attained to the law of righteousness. Wherefore? Because they sought it not by faith, but as it were by the works of the law. For they stumbled at that **stumbling stone**; *As it is written, Behold, I lay in Zion a* **stumbling stone** *and rock of offence: and whosoever believeth on him shall not be ashamed.* (Romans 9:30-33)

As indicated earlier, and borne out by the last of the four verses just quoted, the expression(s) are found in other parts of the Bible. One of these is 1 Corinthians 1:23 where Paul says – "But we preach Christ crucified, *unto the Jews a* **stumbling block**, and unto the Greeks foolishness." This reinforces what he had been saying in Romans chapter 9.

When God instructed Moses in the wider aspects of the law He stated, "Thou shalt not... put a **stumbling block** in the path of the blind." This was from a literal point of view, but more often than not it is used metaphorically to describe an action that causes someone to slip up by not taking a desired course. Sometimes, as with the Lord Jesus, it refers to the person rather than their actions, albeit actions (or words) are at the centre of the matter!

Three brief points in conclusion —

(1) The terms 'stumbling stone' and 'stumbling block' are essentially the same.

(2) Paul gives advice in Romans 14:13 and 1 Corinthians 8:9 about aspects of Christian conduct in order to avoid being a stumbling block to others.

(3) The Lord Jesus of the Bible, who has been divinely called a Stumbling Stone (Isaiah 8:14; 1 Peter 2:8), is also called the Foundation Stone (Isaiah 28:16; 1 Corinthians 3:11) and the Chief Corner Stone of the church universal (Acts 4:11; Ephesians 2:20; 1 Peter 2:6-8).

Chapter 25

Clean gone!

This intriguing saying is found only in Psalm 77:8. Some modern translations substitute the word 'completely' for 'gone'. The sense implies an absoluteness or finality. We will come to all that a little later.

The 150 psalms are divided into five books — 1-41; 42-72; 73-89; 90-106; and 107-150, each closing with a doxology. Psalm 77 falls into the middle section and 11 of these (73-83), together with Psalm 50, are in one way or another ascribed to Asaph. Asaph was a Levite and played an important role in the Temple with regard to the singing.

Psalm 77 is essentially a plea on behalf of a community in a time of great need. Israel and Judah had been carried into captivity (at the instigation of God!). A remnant remained in Jerusalem and it seems Asaph was amongst them and interceding on their behalf.

The Psalm falls into two parts, namely, verses.1-9 and 10-20. The first is largely that of a man looking inwards until he comes to realise that one should more properly consider things from God's perspective. After all, the children of Israel had experienced the goodness of God over and over again, and that He was still in control of the situation; even by bringing about the temporary situation in which they presently found themselves.

Just like ourselves at times, Asaph knew what it was to lie awake at night in despair. He asked a series of questions, all of which could be answered by other scriptures. Here, we confine ourselves to the second question which comprises verse 8 and contains our saying —

*Is his mercy **clean gone** forever? doth his promise fail for evermore?* (Psalm 77:8)

It is important to note that the phrase 'clean gone' is used here from a bad perspective – an apparent failure by God. Things could also be completely gone from a welcoming perspective; for example, a stain on a garment could completely disappear after dry cleaning!

Asaph's use of the word 'is' suggests that he did not accept that God's mercy had failed them, never mind failed them forever! God, being God, surely underlines the impossibility of such a thing. Actually, the answer to his question (or, if you prefer, statement) can be found in such verses as Psalm 30:5 – *'For his anger endureth but a moment; in his favour is life: weeping may endure for a night, but joy cometh in the morning.'*

In one sense Asaph was like Solomon who confined himself to things 'under the sun'. It was only when he looked beyond the sun to the abode of God, and His purposes, did he understand things differently. Similarly, there was a turning point in Asaph's lament. If our sights ever become lowered then, in our hour of need, we must do the same.

Psalm 77 may not be the best known. However, if one studies it in the context of the children of Israel's deliverance out of Egypt and their crossing of the Red Sea etc., then I am convinced that it will be a blessing. Of course, one can draw parallels with their own life experiences. How fitting is this grand old hymn —

Count your many blessings
When upon life's billows you are tempest tossed,
When you are discouraged, thinking all is lost,
Count your many blessings; name them one by one,
And it will surprise you what the Lord hath done.

Refrain
Count your blessings, name them one by one,
Count your blessings, see what God hath done!
Count your blessings, name them one by one,
And it will surprise you what the Lord hath done.

Are you ever burdened with a load of care?
Does the cross seem heavy you are called to bear?
Count your many blessings, every doubt will fly,
And you will keep singing as the days go by.

When you look at others with their lands and gold,
Think that Christ has promised you His wealth
untold; Count your many blessings. Wealth can never
buy Your reward in heaven, nor your home on high.

So, amid the conflict whether great or small,
Do not be disheartened, God is over all;
Count your many blessings, angels will attend,
Help and comfort give you to your journey's end.

*Hold your thumb on this page and flick over to Appendix
1 to get another version of this hymn suitable for singing on
certain occasions!*

Chapter 26

Seeing is believing

If there was ever an expression that required comment then this is one!

The basis for the expression is found in John 20:24-25. The wider background is the earlier verses of the chapter dealing with the resurrection of the Lord Jesus. He had been crucified and raised from (among) the dead as consistently foretold in Scripture.

Before getting into the detail of all that, I must confess that in doing my research I have discovered that the expression is also the title of songs, films, novels and, indeed, an organisation! A quick glance at some of these, as with others in the past, confirms my long term view that there is little in them for anyone, never mind the child of God. Elvis Presley's lyrics of that title, however, are a little more inspiring —

Every time I see the sun rise
Or a mountain that's so high
Just by seeing is believing
I don't need to question why
When I see a mighty ocean
That rushes to the shore

If I ever had cause to doubt Him
I don't doubt Him anymore
Oh seeing, seeing, seeing is believing
And I see Him everywhere
In the mountains, in the valley
Yes I know my God is there
Oh, in time I look above me
See the stars that fill the sky
How could there be any question
Only God can reach that high

In attempting to define the expression, various dictionaries comment along the line that you must see something before you can really believe that it exists. The Cambridge Dictionaries Online states... *it is said to mean that if you see something yourself, you will believe it to exist or be true, despite the fact that it is extremely unusual or unexpected.* This brings us nicely to the context of the saying in John 20:29.

Our blessed Lord Jesus was raised from (among) the dead and seen by a number of persons during the course of the day, including those disciples gathered behind closed doors in fear. One of the twelve disciples, Thomas, was not there. When told about the Lord having appeared to his fellow disciples he exclaimed: *'Except I shall see in his hands the print of the nails, and put my finger into the print of the nails, and thrust my hand into his side, I will not believe.'* (v.25)

The record goes on to relate how that after eight days the disciples were again gathered; this time Thomas with them, the Lord Jesus again coming into their presence and addressing Thomas in the following words: *'Reach hither thy finger, and behold my hands; and reach hither thy hand, and thrust it into my side: and be not faithless, but believing.'* (v.27)

Then comes Thomas' response/reply: *'My Lord and my God.'* (v.28). There is no record of anyone telling the Lord Jesus of Thomas' doubts and demands a week earlier. There was no need to since He is omniscient (all knowing). Equally, there is no record of Thomas having examined either the nail-riven hands or pierced side of his Saviour. Regardless, the Lord Jesus then said to Thomas: *'Thomas, **because thou hast seen me, thou hast believed**: blessed are they that have not seen, and yet have believed.'*

Thomas wanted hard evidence and he got it! The Lord Jesus had previously told His disciples that He was not always going to be on earth. Future converts were not going to have the privilege of seeing Him with the natural eye so, in anticipation of that, and taking account of those, although having not seen the resurrected Lord Jesus but believed in it, He added the words, *'blessed are they that have not seen, and yet have believed.'*

The expression *seeing is believing* stands good, but only for some things. When it comes to the matter of one's salvation it is entirely different. It requires the understanding of certain fundamental facts such as sin, its consequence, the substitutionary death of Christ at Calvary, the need for repentance and then a simple act of faith.

The account of (doubting) Thomas' belief, or rather unbelief, is immediately followed with these words —

And many other signs truly did Jesus in the presence of his disciples, which are not written in this book: <u>But these are written, that ye might believe that Jesus is the Christ, the Son of God; and that believing ye might have life through his name.</u> (John 20:30-31)

It does not say, 'But these are written, that ye **might see** and believe!'

Believe on the Lord Jesus Christ and thou shalt be saved. (Acts 16:31)

Chapter 27

More than enough

This exact phrase is found only in Exodus 36:5. However, the equivalent of it, in rearranged phraseology, is found in the parable of the prodigal son as recorded in Luke's gospel. There is more to the phrase than the customary three words of our expression because the verse in Exodus actually reads **much** *more than enough.*

The word 'enough' on its own is found many times in the Bible. While it usually describes the sufficiency or ampleness of things, it is also used in connection with the insufficiency of things.

If 'enough' indicates sufficiency, and 'more than enough' that bit extra, then 'much more than enough' surely suggests super abundance! Two verses further on (Exodus 36:7) in the same chapter supports this thought. It may be useful at this point to quote all three verses (5, 6 & 7) —

*And they spake unto Moses, saying, The people bring <u>much</u> **more than enough** for the service of the work, which the Lord commanded to make.*
And Moses gave commandment, and they caused it to be proclaimed throughout the camp, saying, Let neither man nor woman make any more work for the offering of the sanctuary. So the people were restrained from bringing.
For the stuff they had was <u>sufficient</u> for all the work to make it, <u>and too much</u>. (Underscoring and other emphasis added.)

Now may be the time to introduce the supporting verse from Luke's gospel —

*And when he came to himself, he said, How many hired servants of my father's have bread **enough and to spare**, and I perish with hunger! (Luke 15:17).*

Exodus chapters 19 through 40 deal with the arrival of the children of Israel at Sinai (after their deliverance from Egypt), Moses' meeting with God there on the Mount, the giving of the moral law (Ten Commandments), the ceremonial law, instructions concerning the building of the tabernacle, the priesthood, the priestly garments and much more. The level of detail shows that nothing was left to the imagination.

Exodus 25:1 onwards is the record of the Lord's command regarding the supply of the materials for the Tabernacle —

And the Lord spake unto Moses, saying, Speak unto the children of Israel, that they bring me an offering: of <u>every man that giveth it</u> <u>willingly with his heart</u> ye shall take my offering. And this is the offering which ye shall take of them; gold, and silver, and brass.... (Underscoring added)

Ten chapters further on (35:4) we have the account of Moses' compliance with that command and in verses 21-29 the children of Israel's overwhelming response. Then, in the chapter that follows, we have the 'complaint' from the builders regarding the excess of supplies, which brings us directly to the verses containing our expression (36:5-7).

Take time to read the chapters for yourself. Note well the repeated words 'willing-hearted' and such like.

And one final thought. There is no mention of garden fetes, church car boot sales or other fundraising events as a means of meeting the needs associated with God's house.

Chapter 28

Little by little

This expression simply means: *gradually*, or *a bit at a time.*

The basis for the expression is the rearranged words 'by little and little' as found in Exodus 23:30 and Deuteronomy 7:22. Both refer to the same occasion – God on Mount Sinai giving instruction to Moses regarding the children of Israel's conquest of the Promised Land. Exodus is the original account, and Deuteronomy a restatement (with minor additions), partly due to a new generation of people.

Exodus 23:30 and Deuteronomy 7:22 both read —

By little and little *I will drive them out from before thee, until thou be increased, and inherit the land.*

As stated in the previous chapter, the children of Israel have been delivered out of Egypt and have now reached Sinai. Moses has been called up into the Mount to meet with God. Through him God enters into a covenant with His people. The Ten Commandments on two tablets of stone are given, as were a number of other laws. Following that were the instructions concerning the keeping of three national feasts, and then the instructions concerning the entering into the Promised Land [Canaan] (Exodus 23:20-33).

God promised to send an angel to lead them and drive out the heathen inhabitants. They would be given the land bit by bit and, in the process, they were not to intermingle with the inhabitants or involve themselves in idolatry etc. God, in all His wisdom, knew they could not take proper control of the land since they had insufficient numbers. Had the others been driven out all at once the children of Israel would have been overrun with wild beasts.

In the last decade or so there have been many examples of this type of dilemma. While no one would approve of the actions of despots, we have seen uprisings that got out of control causing as many problems as they have solved. At least, when under dictatorship, those situations did not exist!

Returning to things spiritual we make one final observation. God's 'little by little' plan for the possession of the land was no half baked measure. Similarly, God has not dealt with us in part measure with regard to our sin. The price was paid in full through the sacrificial, sin atoning death of His Son at Calvary. A number of verses come to mind —

As far as the east is from the west, so far hath he removed our transgressions from us. (Psalm 103:12)

And their sins and iniquities will I remember no more. (Hebrews 10:17)

The blood of Jesus Christ, God's Son, cleanseth us from all sin. (1 John 1:7)

Chapter 29

To tell you the truth

This is an interesting expression in that it can mean anything from 'being honest' to 'being frank', to 'saying what you really think' even to 'admitting to something'! It differs slightly from the *to tell you the gospel truth* expression which is dealt with in the next chapter.

Telling the truth can have wider implications than just honesty! Sometimes it can lead to the loss of a friend, as will be seen from the Galatians 4:16 verse further down.

There is also the humorous side to the use of the expression. Someone might be talking for a period of time and then suddenly introduces the phrase, *to tell you the truth,* and continues talking. This often results in the hearer interrupting to say, 'Does that mean that everything else you have said until now was not the truth?'

Then there is the case of a well-known figure in Northern Ireland who attended a public enquiry stating that he was there to tell the truth. However, within no time at all he refused to answer certain questions that he had been asked which demanded the truth!

During trial by Pilate, the Lord Jesus said, *'for this cause came I into the world, that I should bear witness unto the truth.'* This begged Pilate to ask, *'What is truth?'* before immediately going out from His presence without waiting for the answer! Nevertheless, he immediately addressed the Saviour's Jewish accusers and exclaimed, *'I find in him no fault at all.'* How could he have said anything else? Only a few hours earlier in the Upper Room the Lord Jesus told Thomas (and the other disciples) – *'I am the way, **the truth**, and the life: no man cometh unto the Father, but by me.'*

Of the 237 occurrences of the word 'truth' in the Bible the Lord Jesus spoke it more than 25 times. Of the three occurrences of the phrase, *I tell you the truth*, the Lord Jesus spoke it on two of the occasions; the first in John 8:45 to the antagonistic, unbelieving Jews, and the second time, to His disciples in the Upper Room (John 16:7). On two other occasions, Luke 4:26 and Luke 9:27, He used a slight variation of the phrase – *I tell you of a truth* where the emphasis seems to be on the introduction of a new truth, rather than on the veracity of it.

The three verses containing the, *I tell you the truth,* phrase are —

John 8:45
*And because **I tell you the truth**, ye believe me not.*

John *15:7*
*Nevertheless **I tell you the truth;** It is expedient for you that I go away: for if I go not away, the Comforter will not come unto you; but if I depart, I will send him unto you.*

Galatians 4:16
*Am I therefore become your enemy, because **I tell you the truth?***

In conclusion, the Lord Jesus is the one Person who could have spoken without the need to use the words of our saying in the way that we tend to use them of ourselves today!

Chapter 30

The gospel truth

What a lovely expression we have here. It differs from that covered in our previous chapter in that it is used, not just to indicate the truth, but to emphasize it. In other words, it is stressing that what has been said is as undeniable as the gospel itself.

There is a sense, however, in which users of the expression have little or no idea as to what it really means, nor have they ever entered into the good of it. That is what we now hope to clarify.

Some like to quote John 3:16 and refer to it as 'the gospel in a nutshell' —

For God so loved the world, that he gave his only begotten Son, that whosoever believeth in him should not perish, but have everlasting life.

Personally, I like to combine it with 1 Corinthians 15:1-4 which read —

... the gospel which I preached unto you, ...how that Christ died for our sins according to the scriptures; And that he was buried, and that he rose again the third day according to the scriptures.

As a matter of interest, read the 1 Corinthians 15 verses in full and notice, in a day when so many are questioning the bodily resurrection of the Lord Jesus, that the apostle Paul actually uses the gospel to prove the resurrection!

Four verses which contain our expression in the form of rearranged words or, if you prefer, the basis for it, are —

Galatians 2:5
*... that **the truth of the gospel** might continue with you.*

Galatians 2:14
*... they walked not uprightly according to **the truth of the gospel**,...*

Ephesians 1:13
*In whom ye also trusted, after that ye heard **the word of truth, the gospel** of your salvation: in whom also after that ye believed...*

Colossians 1:5
*For the hope which is laid up for you in heaven, whereof ye heard before in **the word of the truth of the gospel;***

Other interesting facts about this gospel are —

The Lord Jesus taught it. Matthew 4:23
The disciples were to proclaim it. Mark 16:15
Paul was not ashamed of it; neither should we be. Romans 1:16
Paul preached it; and so must we. 1 Corinthians 1:23
Paul defended it; and so must we. Philippians 1:17
Many believed it; and so did I. Acts 4:4
Some were thankful for it; and so should we be. Colossians 1:3-5
Some perverted it; we must never. Galatians 1:6-12
Some disobeyed it; see below. Romans 2:8

2 Thessalonians 1:8 states: *the Lord will appear from heaven with His mighty angels in flaming fire, taking vengeance on them that know not God and obey not the gospel of our Lord Jesus Christ.*

1 Peter 4:17 asks: *What shall the end be of them that obey not the gospel of God?*

Chapter 31

Sour grapes

It was during my research for the saying in the next chapter that I came across the words 'sour grape' (more properly translated 'sour grapes', plural) and wondered if they had anything to do with our everyday expression *sour grapes*. That set me off on a tangent and I was encouraged to see that one website indicated that it was an allusion to Jeremiah 31:29 – the exact verse where I noticed it! We will get to this, and other verses, shortly.

The dictionary.com website defines sour grapes as: *pretended disdain for something one does not or cannot have* and goes on to give a sample phrase – *She said that she and her husband didn't want to join the club anyway, but it was clearly sour grapes*.

That interpretation is illustrated by the fable of The Fox and the Grapes: *Driven by hunger, a fox tried to reach some grapes hanging high on the vine but was unable to, although he leaped with all his strength. As he went away, the fox remarked, 'Oh, you aren't even ripe yet! I don't need any of your sour grapes.'*

It seems, however, that the expression is also used in a resentful way towards people as well as things. For example, where neighbours have fallen out over the height of a boundary hedge one might subsequently criticise the other's new garden gate design, not because they do not like it, but because of the animosity existing between them.

The words 'sour grape' are found in Isaiah 18:5, Jeremiah 31:29,30 (where they should be more properly translated in the plural), and Ezekiel 18:2 (where they are in the plural). With the exception of the Isaiah usage, all are obviously linked to our saying in some way or another. It is interesting to note that the verse in Ezekiel 18:2 clearly states that the words were part of a proverb! The Jeremiah verse tends to suggest that too. Jeremiah 31:29 and 30 read —

In those days they shall say no more, The fathers have eaten **a sour grape,** *and the children's teeth are set on edge. But everyone shall die for his own iniquity: every man that eateth the* **sour grape,** *his teeth shall be set on edge.*

Ezekiel 18:2 reads —

What mean ye, that ye use this proverb concerning the land of Israel, saying, The fathers have eaten **sour grapes,** *and the children's teeth are set on edge?*

It seems that the proverb referred to was commonplace at that time. The eating of the sour grapes is most likely allegorical. We know how bitter the taste of any sour fruit is, and how upsetting it might be.

Among other things, Jeremiah prophesied regarding the destruction of Jerusalem, Judah's exile in Babylon, their restoration in the short and long terms, and the New Covenant. He did not go into exile.

Ezekiel, for a period overlapped, and then followed Jeremiah. He was himself carried into Babylonian captivity and prophesied concerning the whole house of Israel. Amongst other things, he reminded those born during the captivity that although it was the national sins of their fathers that led to the captivity, nonetheless, they themselves would be punished for personal sins unless they repented. It is against that background that the phrase 'sour grapes', then in common use, was taken up and commented upon by the prophets.

It is nothing new for people to be in a state of denial. Judah was no exception. The younger generation could not see the mote in their own eye. They blamed their forefathers for the fact that they were now in captivity. And they were right! Read Exodus 20 verse 5 *(...for I the Lord thy God am a jealous God, visiting the iniquity of the fathers upon the children unto the third and fourth generation of them that hate me...*) But that was only half the story. They were sinful too, and unless they repented they would meet the same righteous judgment of God.

The proverb was being used as a lame excuse for their own sinful condition and, now that the record was put straight, they were to no longer use it.

It may be difficult to fully reconcile today's use of the *sour grapes* expression with its biblical use. Nevertheless, I trust your appetite has been whetted for further study.

Judah had to be reminded, in the very same breath, that God stated that the soul that sinneth shall die.

Both prophets told of a coming day at the end of the Great Tribulation when Christ would return to earth and execute judgment in righteousness. Repentant Israel would see their mistake and no longer use the expression.

Chapter 32

Took him/her/them by the hand

This expression, in the context of use as an everyday saying, is found only twice in the Bible (Jeremiah 31:32 and Hebrews 8:9). The latter verse is merely the reciting of the former! Its equivalent, *taking them by the arms* is also found in Hosea 11:3.

There is no doubt that the use of the phrase in the biblical setting, and today, is figurative; unlike the healing of Peter's mother-in-law (Mark 1:31), the raising of Jairus' daughter from the dead (Mark 5:41, Luke 8:54) and the healing of the lame man in Acts 3:1-11 where it was literal.

When we use the expression figuratively it simply means 'to guide someone'. When someone needs a word of advice we might say, take him (aside) by the arm and have a (wee) word (of advice) in his ear! Alternatively, we might say, 'so and so would not be where he is today only for me taking him by the hand when he was staring up and showing him how to really run a business.'

As the writer to the Hebrews progresses through his epistle he has occasion to compare and contrast the Old and New covenants. In doing so he quotes the words of the Lord as found in Jeremiah 31:31-34. Rather than duplicating them here we will restrict ourselves to the Jeremiah passage, and only the first two verses at that —

*Behold, the days come, saith the Lord, that I will make a new covenant with the house of Israel, and with the house of Judah: Not according to the covenant that I made with their fathers in the day that I **took them by the hand** to bring them out of the land of Egypt; which my covenant they brake, although I was an husband unto them, saith the Lord. (*Jeremiah 31:31-32)

Something of the prophecies of Jeremiah has been outlined in our previous chapter. I am glad to say that the verses containing our current expression (and which immediately follow the verses containing our previous saying) are more easily understood.

The Lord is dealing with the superiority of a new (unconditional) covenant — at that time still to be made — over that of the old (conditional) covenant that existed when he led the children of Israel out of Egypt, and which they broke. Had it not been for the Lord taking them by the hand, so to speak, leading and guiding them, they never would have made it!

The same sentiments are expressed in Hosea 11:3 – *I taught Ephraim also to go, taking them by their arms.* (Ephraim is one of the names by which the northern tribes of Israel were known due to it being the largest of those tribes.)

We conclude with a chorus which my mother got to know (and love) in later life. I wonder (or do I), if the phrase 'When He takes me by the hand' in the refrain is literal or figurative!

There is coming a day
When no heartaches shall come
No more clouds in the sky
No more tears to dim the eye
All is peace forevermore
On that happy golden shore
What a day, glorious day that will be!

What a day that will be
When my Jesus I shall see
And I look upon His face
The One who saved me by His grace
When He takes me by the hand
And leads me through the Promised Land,
What a day, glorious day that will be!

There'll be no sorrow there
No more burdens to bear
No more sickness, no pain
No more parting over there
And forever I will be
With the One who died for me
What a day, glorious day that will be!

What a day that will be
When my Jesus I shall see
And I look upon His face
The One who saved me by His grace
When He takes me by the hand
And leads me through the Promised Land,
What a day, glorious day that will be!

Chapter 33

The apple of my eye

Upwards of ten million hits on Google for various forms of this phrase tell us something of the interest in it.

Just recently I was in conversation with a friend who, speaking of another person, remarked, 'She's a sweetheart.' He said it with sincerity, and even went on to repeat it! My heart was touched. He was not speaking in the romantic sense of which the word is often used but, rather, of the personal qualities that the lady possessed.

Delightful and all as the sweetheart expression is, it falls short of the one under consideration. Used figuratively, *the apple of my eye* expression describes something, or more often, someone, who is cherished above others. This is true of the occasions where the phrase is used in the Bible.

But first, I understand the expression was originally an anatomical term. The central part (pupil), the most precious part of the eye, was likened to an apple because of its shape. With that in mind, and knowing from as early as Genesis chapter 12 that God chose the Jew/Israel to be his special earthly people/nation (note well the word, <u>earthly</u>), is it any wonder that the expression, *the apple of his eye,* has been used to describe them and thus become a metaphor!

Just as an aside, it has often been debated whether total blindness or total deafness is the worse. Based on the preciousness of the eye, and God's prerogative to describe His special earthly people after that organ part, I can only conclude that blindness must be the worse.

The five occasions where we find 'the apple of the eye' expression (or minor variants) are —

Deuteronomy 32:10

*He found him in a desert land, and in the waste howling wilderness; he led him about, he instructed him, he kept him as **the apple of his eye.***

Psalms 17:8

*Keep me as **the apple of the eye**; hide me under the shadow of thy wings.*

Proverbs 7:2

*Keep my commandments, and live; and my law as **the apple of thine eye.***

Lamentations 2:18

*Their heart cried unto the Lord, O wall of the daughter of Zion, let tears run down like a river day and night: give thyself no rest; let not **the apple of thine eye** cease.*

Zachariah 2:8

*For thus saith the Lord of hosts; After the glory hath he sent me unto the nations which spoiled you: for he that toucheth you toucheth **the apple of his eye.***

Psalms 17:8 and Proverbs 7:2 are the odd ones out. They are not exclusive to the nation of Israel; the other three are. Psalm 17 is a prayer of David for deliverance and Proverbs 7 is Solomon's plea for obedience to his commandments.

And a quick comment on Zachariah 2:8 in closing; the touching of the (apple of the) eye is the equivalent of what we would today call 'a poke in the eye'! God's chosen earthly people, Israel, despite having been poked in the eye (attacked) over and over again, have survived against all natural odds! And survive they must. God is faithful, and will carry out all that He has promised. Hints of this are found elsewhere in this book.

Chapter 34

In the land of the living

Today, this expression tends to be used humorously and, being of the jovial type myself, I use it regularly. Sometimes I use it towards a person whom I have not seen for a long time and/or, perhaps, one who has returned home after a long absence. At other times I direct it teasingly toward persons of a grand old age — apparently surprised that they are still alive. (I can see some of my older friends smiling at this very moment!)

Of course, in the same humorous vein, it is sometimes used to describe persons who have awakened from sleep; whether after a brief doze, a prolonged sleep, or at an unusual hour.

As with many of our sayings, the expression has found its way into novel, song and film titles etc.

The expression *land of the living* is found 15 times in the Bible. They are all in the Old Testament and, in one particular chapter they are in five succeeding verses! With the exception of Ezekiel 26:20, Ezekiel 32:23, 24, 25, 26, 27 and 32, which will be dealt with collectively, the remaining eight are listed below —

Job 28:12-14

But where shall wisdom be found? and where is the place of understanding?

*Man knoweth not the price thereof; neither is it found **in the land of the living.***
The depth saith, It is not in me: and the sea saith, It is not with me.

Note: Job is dealing with the search for wisdom. Not only does he declare that it cannot be obtained from man anywhere on earth, but that the price (worth of it in non monetary terms) is also not within man's knowledge.

Psalm 27:13
*I had fainted, unless I had believed to see the goodness of the Lord **in the land of the living.***

Psalm 52:5
*God shall likewise destroy thee forever, he shall take thee away, and pluck thee out of thy dwelling place, and root thee out of **the land of the living**. Selah.*

(The 'root out' expression in the verse is dealt with in chapter 2.)

Psalm 116:9
*I will walk before the Lord **in the land of the living.***

Psalm 142:5
*I cried unto thee, O Lord: I said, Thou art my refuge and my portion **in the land of the living.***

Isaiah 38:11
*I said, I shall not see the Lord, even the Lord, **in the land of the living:** I shall behold man no more with the inhabitants of the world.*

Isaiah 53:8
*He was taken from prison and from judgment: and who shall declare his generation? for he was cut off out of **the land of the living**: for the transgression of my people was he stricken.*

Jeremiah 11:19
But I was like a lamb or an ox that is brought to the slaughter; and I knew not that they had devised devices against me, saying,

Let us destroy the tree with the fruit thereof, and let us cut him off from **the land of the living**, *that his name may be no more remembered.*

In all of the above instances *the land of the living* simply means the earth, or, if you prefer, from those who were alive on earth. On some occasions the emphasis seems to be on the more local scene.

The remaining seven references are contained in that middle section of Ezekiel's prophecy sandwiched between those sections which deal with (1) his own exiled people before the final siege of Jerusalem (Chs 1-24), and (2) Judah's final fall (Chs 33-48).

Ezekiel, at the time of the siege of Jerusalem, turns his attention to seven neighbouring Gentile nations (Ammon, Moab, Edom, Philistia, Tyre, Sidon and Egypt) and prophecies of their doom. They were no friends of Judah and had taken great delight in what had happened to her.

Chapters 25-32 detail the varying degrees of punishment that would be imposed — displacement of inhabitants, death and utter destruction of cities, etc — and illustrate the point by listing a number of former nations (Ch 32) that were similarly dealt with. They had caused much terror amongst those with whom they lived but now they were a people of the past. God dealt with them in righteous judgment.

Chapter 35

Wits' end!

Unlike the previous saying, which features 15 times in the Bible, *wits' end* is found only once (Psalm 107:27). One website attributes its origin to the Bible.

The Cambridge dictionary defines it as: *to be so worried, confused, or annoyed that you do not know what to do next* and goes on to give the example – *I'm at my wits' end. I don't know how to help him.*

Most authorities suggest there is little difference between this expression and that of being *at the end of one's tether.*

In connection with an earlier saying we stated that the Psalms are divided into five sections or books; the latter being Psalms 107-150 and that those final 44 Psalms are essentially Psalms of the Captivity and Return to Jerusalem. It is the first of those Psalms that contains the verse with our present saying —

*They reel to and fro, and stagger like a drunken man, and are at their **wits' end.*** (Psalm 107:27)

The Psalm speaks of God's provision for the redeemed and opens with a call for thanksgiving because of the Lord's goodness and mercy. That call is repeated four times at the end of sections dealing with four different classes of people: those that have lost their way (4-9); those that have lost their freedom (10-16); those that have lost their health (17-22), and those who have lost hope (23-32). Doubtless, these verses could describe the children of Israel in their wanderings in the desert right through to their ultimate redemption at the end times.

The imagery in verses 23-27 describing seafarers in the midst of a huge storm is most striking. Not only is the ship tossed to and fro, but, so too, its crew. They stagger about like a drunken man; they are at their wits' end not knowing what to do next, hence our expression.

Struggles of great magnitude can face us all, not just seafarers. These can be family, financial, health or work related etc. Christians are not exempt and in some situations Satan can have a heyday. At times we just do not know where to turn.

I am not a qualified counsellor and thus restricted in what I can advise in many of these situations. However, professional advice can often be complemented with the words of a little chorus I learned well over 30 years ago —

Christ is the answer to my every need
Christ is the answer He is my Friend indeed
Problems of life my spirit may assail
With Christ my Saviour I need never fail
For Christ is the answer to my need!

On a humorous note, I recall singing the above words at the top of my voice (soon after learning it all those years ago) as I rode my motor cycle to work at 6 o'clock in the morning. The cows in the field seemed bemused at the sound and I doubt if it did anything to increase the milk yield!

Brief mention was made earlier to *the end of one's tether* expression so, in conclusion, here is a lovely slogan that I read recently —

When you feel that you're at the end of your tether,
remember that God is at the other end!

Chapter 36

Pride comes/goes before a fall

Of the many everyday sayings covered in this book, including those in its companion volume, I hazard to guess that this saying is possibly the best known and the most understood.

It is essential that we understand the meaning of the words 'pride' and 'fall' before we examine the complete expression. Simple.m.wikipedia.org has the following posting on pride which is reproduced in full with permission —

Pride means having a feeling of being good and worthy. The adjective is proud.

The word pride can be used in a good sense as well as in a bad sense.

In a good sense it means having a feeling of self-respect. People can be satisfied with their achievements. They can be proud of something good that they have done. They can be proud of (or take pride in) their work. They might be proud of their son or daughter or husband or wife or anyone else who is close to them and who has done something good. People can be proud of their country (patriotism).

The opposite would be to be ashamed of someone or something.

In a bad sense, pride can mean that someone has an exaggerated sense of feeling good. This might mean that someone has no respect for what other people do, only respect for what he or she does. Someone who is described as proud may be arrogant. The word is used   in   this   sense   in   the saying: "Pride comes before a fall" (meaning that someone is so overconfident that he or she might soon have a disaster).

Fall, in the context of our expression, means downfall or ruin.

The basis for the expression *pride comes/goes before a fall* is found in Proverbs 16:18 —

Pride goeth *before destruction, and an haughty spirit before* **a fall**.

On the other hand, and based on the meaning of the two key words, it could be argued that the expression is found twice in the verse in the form of a synonymous parallelism! (See chapter 14 for an explanation of what this means.)

The verse is not an isolated one on the subject; verses 5 and 19 of the same chapter and Proverbs 29:23 are in support. They read —

Every one that is proud in heart is an abomination to the Lord: though hand join in hand, he shall not be unpunished. (Proverbs 16:5)

Better it is to be of an humble spirit with the lowly, than to divide the spoil with the proud. (Proverbs 16:19)

A man's pride shall bring him low: but honour shall uphold the humble in spirit. (Proverbs 29:23)

It is important to note the closeness of the time between the moment of pride and the fall. It is sooner rather than later; in fact almost immediately. A good example of this is found in Daniel chapter 4 concerning the boastful pride of King Nebuchadnezzar. Despite his dream being interpreted for him he continued on in his own arrogant way. He had the audacity to walk in the palace of the kingdom of Babylon and proclaim, '*Is not this great Babylon that I have built for the house of the kingdom by the might of* **my power,** *and for* **the honour of my** *majesty?'* No sooner had he said it when there came a voice from heaven to tell him that he would lose it all. The passage goes on to state that the pronouncement was fulfilled in the same hour!

The same principle can be seen in that prophesied of the Antichrist in a coming day. He 'exalted himself above all' and sits in the temple declaring himself to be God (2 Thessalonians 2:4). As stated earlier in connection with another saying, God will make short work of him.

There is also the parable of the rich fool in Luke chapter 12 who said, *'And I will say to my soul, Soul, thou hast much goods laid up for many years; take thine ease, eat, drink, and be merry. But God said unto him, Thou fool, **this night** thy soul shall be required of thee: then whose shall those things be, which thou hast provided?'* There are many more examples, including those in our own day.

Note also that Proverbs 16:5 stresses the seriousness of pride when it states that it is an abomination to the Lord. (Incidentally, the word abomination is found 77 times in the Authorised Version of our Bible; Old and New Testaments alike.) The consequences are made clear in Psalm 138:6 – *'Though the Lord be high, yet hath he respect unto the lowly: but the proud he knoweth afar off.'*

Despite the saying being exceptionally well known, and even understood, it is a fact that many still succumb to pride! Indeed, pride in the good sense as described earlier, can soon turn to pride in the bad sense. Self control is required to combat it and, thankfully, for the believer this is one of the fruit of the Spirit listed in Galatians chapter 5. The opposite of pride is humility (meekness) and this is similarly listed in the fruit of the Spirit.

Is it any wonder that Paul writing to the believers in Rome pleaded, *'be not conformed to this world: but be ye transformed by the renewing of your mind, that ye may prove what is that good, and acceptable, and perfect, will of God... not to think of himself more highly than he ought to think; but to think soberly...'* (12:2-3).

It is interesting to note that Satan, who is the master hand of this pride, fell foul of it himself. He was privileged to be in Heaven with God but this went to his head with the result that he, and a third of the other angels, were cast out for ever. That is a big subject in itself and beyond our study here. However, are we not glad of the Scripture which says, *'He hath not dealt with us after our sins; nor rewarded us according to our iniquities.'* (Psalm 103:10)

Hopefully sufficient has been said to whet your appetite for further study. We close with two other sayings pertaining to pride —

No one ever choked swallowing his/her pride!

Temper gets you into trouble. Pride keeps you there!

Chapter 37

Right-hand man

This expression has been variously described as: *an indispensable helper, chief assistant, the most helpful assistant, a trusted helper.* All such descriptions, of course, could equally apply to women.

One dictionary suggests that the right-hand man expression is derived from the accounts of Jesus sitting on the right hand of God. However, there is at least one earlier reference in the Bible to the right-hand man and we will come to this later.

Unlike the introductory descriptions, the reference to Jesus sitting on the right hand of God, as we will see shortly, is symbolic and denotes honour, power and authority. Exodus 15:6 illustrates the point — *'Thy right hand, O LORD, has become glorious in power; Thy right hand, O LORD, has dashed the enemy in pieces.'* There are numerous other verses in support.

Mindful that we have just dealt with pride in the previous chapter, I dare to introduce a little humour here. Many years ago I was appointed to a relatively important (and enjoyable) position and subsequently underwent a media training course. Under the glare of the camera and an assembled audience, and, in an attempt to unsettle me, the interviewer suggested that I was 'the hatchet man'. In order to get out of a tight spot I simply agreed and that put an end to that particular line of questioning! In some ways the expression hatchet man is unkind, but I leave you to consider whether elements of it have anything in common with the *right- hand man* saying we are discussing.

Despite all that has been said, the precise phrase 'right-hand man' is not found in the Bible although the basis for it is. As with some of the other sayings, it is merely a re-ordering of words.

Before picking out a few verses for comment I just mention that the name Benjamin means 'son of my right hand'.

All four Gospel accounts must be studied in order to get the fullest account of the arrest, trial and crucifixion of the Lord Jesus. However, it is the synoptic accounts that deal with His appearance before the Sanhedrin and His being questioned as to His Messiahship and deity. While all three record His reply *(...the Son of man sitting on the right hand of power)*, it is Luke's account which clarifies it by adding the words, *of God*, (Luke 22:69). As suggested earlier, power is the central consideration.

Matthew and Mark's parallel accounts (Matthew 26:24; Mark 14:62) read —

*Jesus saith unto him, Thou hast said: nevertheless I say unto you, Hereafter shall ye see **the Son of man sitting on the right hand of power**, and coming in the clouds of heaven.*

Commenting on this in the Believer's Bible Commentary, the beloved William MacDonald states, *In essence He was saying, "I am the Christ, the Son of God, as you have said. My glory is presently veiled in a human body; I appear to be just another man. You see Me in the days of My humiliation. But the day is coming when you Jews will see Me as the glorified One, equal in all respects with God, sitting at His right hand and coming on the clouds of heaven."*

I am convinced there is much more to this verse than meets the eye. Again, the 'sitting' is most likely metaphorical and took place upon the Lord's ascension, and the 'coming' refers to both the rapture and subsequent return to earth in judgment. However, as already suggested, the emphasis is on the position of honour, power and authority – at God's right hand.

The same thought is expressed in Hebrews 10:12, where dealing with the superiority of Christ's sacrifice, it is said —

*But **this man**, after he had offered one sacrifice for sins for ever, **sat down on the right hand of God**.*

and Acts 7:55, 56, where Stephen, in his martyrdom —

*Being full of the Holy Ghost, looked up steadfastly into heaven, and saw the glory of God, **and Jesus standing on the right hand of God,** And said, Behold, I see the heavens opened, **and the Son of man standing on the right hand of God.***

Comment has often been passed on the 'standing' in these verses as opposed to the 'sitting' in the other verses. It is suggested that the 'standing' here indicates the Saviour's readiness to receive Stephen's spirit.

Two further verses from the Psalms will suffice. Psalm 80 is the prayer of Asaph crying unto the Lord for a resumption of His favour toward wayward Israel. At the close he acknowledges that this is possible through the Man of His right hand. It is clear from Psalm 110:1, Hebrews 1:3, Hebrews 8:1 and Hebrews 10:12 that this Man is the Lord Jesus Christ. Psalm 80:17 reads —

*Let thy hand be upon **the man of thy right hand**, upon the son of man whom thou madest strong for thyself.*

Psalm 142:4 reads —

*I looked on my **right hand**, and beheld, but there was no **man** that would know me: refuge failed me; no **man** cared for my soul.*

This was part of a prayer of David when he was seeking refuge in a cave. He poured his heart out before God and told Him that when he looked to his right he found no man to help him. This verse is different from the others that contain our expression in that it highlights the absence of a right-hand man.

David may not have had a right-hand man on earth to turn to at that time. However, as can be seen from the very same Psalm (and others) he was able to turn to the Lord. Hebrews 4:14-16 remind us of the Great High Priest to whom we can turn —

Seeing then that we have a great high priest, that is passed into the heavens, Jesus the Son of God, let us hold fast our profession. For we have not an high priest which cannot be touched with the feeling of our infirmities; but was in all points tempted like as we are, yet without sin. Let us therefore come boldly unto the throne of grace that we may obtain mercy, and find grace to help in time of need.

In addition, although in a different context, the Apostle John in his first epistle (1 John 2:1) reminds us —

And if any man sin, we have an advocate with the Father, Jesus Christ the righteous.

Advocacy is surely another characteristic of someone who is a right-hand man.

I finish with a hymn that I have recently got to know and love. I trust that it will be a blessing to you —

Does Jesus Care?
Does Jesus care when my heart is pained,
Too deeply for mirth or song,
As the burdens press, and the cares distress,
And the way grows weary and long?

Refrain
Oh, yes, He cares, I know He cares,
His heart is touched with my grief;
When the days are weary, the long nights dreary,
I know my Saviour cares.

Does Jesus care when my way is dark,
With a nameless dread and fear?
As the daylight fades into deep night shades,
Does He care enough to be near?

Does Jesus care when I've tried and failed,
To resist some temptation strong;
When for my deep grief there is no relief,
Though my tears flow all the night long?

Does Jesus care when I've said "goodbye,"
To the dearest on earth to me,
And my sad heart aches till it nearly breaks—
Is it aught to Him? Does He see?

Chapter 38

See eye to eye

This expression is found only once in the Bible and has a meaning completely different to that generally associated with it today. In the Bible it is used literally (something akin to 'face to face') whereas in common usage today it is used metaphorically.

When used metaphorically the expression means to agree with someone; in other words, be likeminded. It is different from the expressions *look someone in the eye/face* (meaning directly and forthrightly, and supposedly, with honesty) and *catch someone's eye* (meaning, to get their attention).

Our expression, as already indicated, is found only in Isaiah 52:8. However, before turning to that verse in particular a quick word about the book in general may help.

The book of Isaiah has often been described as a miniature Bible. It has 66 chapters while the Bible has 66 books. The first 39 chapters of Isaiah correspond to the 39 books of the Old Testament which largely anticipate the coming of (the) Messiah. The last 27 chapters of Isaiah mirror the 27 chapters of the New Testament in that they speak a great deal about (the) Messiah and His Kingdom as the Servant of the Lord. Chapters 1-39 speak of man's great need of salvation while chapters 40-66 reveal God's provision of Salvation in (the) Messiah and His kingdom.

The King James Study Bible divides the last 27 chapters into three groups of nine and ascribes the following headings: 40-48, *Purpose of Peace;* 49-57, *Prince of Peace;* 58-66, *Program of Peace.* The centre group has chapter 53 at its centre!

The key word in the book is 'salvation' (66 times) and key verses include 7:14; 9:6-7; 53:4-7. As inferred, perhaps the best known chapter is 53 which is often read in conjunction with the closing verses of chapter 52 – just a few verses on from the one containing our expression —

*Thy watchmen shall lift up the voice; with the voice together shall they sing: for they shall **see eye to eye,** when the Lord shall bring again Zion.* (Isaiah 52:8)

The background to the saying is this; Judah had been in captivity and suffered greatly. They were about to be set free. Their failures have been forgiven (Ch 51). They were free to return. In chapter 52 the remnant in Zion (Jerusalem) were given a wake-up call and told how to behave. They were to sound the good news and the city's watchmen were to be on the lookout for them. The moment that they saw them come near (eye to eye) they were to rejoice with singing.

While some parts of the prophecy were fulfilled when Judah returned from Babylon the wider application is to Israel in their final restoration at the end times. Some commentators (erringly) apply these chapters to the church (God's heavenly people) rather than Israel (God's earthly people).

In our opening paragraph we mentioned that the *see eye to eye* expression was in ways similar to the *face to face* expression. The latter reminds me a lovely hymn —

Face to face with Christ my Saviour,
Face to face, what will it be?
When with rapture I behold Him,
Jesus Christ who died for me?

Refrain
Face to face I shall behold Him,
Far beyond the starry sky;
Face to face in all His glory,
I shall see Him by and by!

Only faintly now I see Him
With the darkened veil between,
But a blessed day is coming
When His glory shall be seen.

What rejoicing in His presence,
When are banished grief and pain;
When the crooked ways are straightened,
And the dark things shall be plain.

Face to face, oh blissful moment!
Face to face, to see and know;
Face to face, with my Redeemer,
Jesus Christ who loves me so.

(Words by Carrie E. Breck, 1898)

Chapter 39

Two-edged sword / double edged sword

The expression *two-edged sword* is found four times in the Bible; twice in the Old Testament and twice in the New Testament. Its equivalent, *(sharp) sword with two edges* is found a few verses further on from the last of these four in the book of Revelation where there are a number of references to the sword.

An ordinary sword, and for that matter, a double-edged sword, need little defining. The latter, with both edges sharp, cuts both ways. This might help us understand some of the metaphorical usages of the phrase in the Bible.

In addition to its literal meaning, and as just indicated, it is also used metaphorically with the following meanings: (1) something that can be understood or interpreted in two ways, thus a double-edged remark, (2) having or able to have both desirable and undesirable results, the latter not always being immediately apparent. I must confess that I never associated the first of these interpretations with the expression!

We now examine each of the verses where the expression is found and comment accordingly —

Psalm 149:6
*Let the high praises of God be in their mouth, and a **two-edged sword** in their hand;*

Comment: this might be an allusion to what happened during the rebuilding of the walls in Jerusalem (Nehemiah 4:17). The usage here is metaphorical. In its broadest sense this refers to the end times when God will establish His kingdom on the earth. Spiritual Israel will have occasion to glorify God and, at the same time, execute judgment upon the wicked. This must be done in accordance with the written word of

God; governing properly, yet defending the rights of people, thus indicating the double/two-edged element of the phrase – where the emphasis seems to lie.

This penultimate Psalm has only 9 verses so take time to read it in full.

Proverbs 5:4
*But her end is bitter as wormwood, sharp as a **two-edged sword.***

Comment: Solomon is here warning against immorality. The consequences are far reaching and have the same destructive effect as a two-edged sword. Again, usage is metaphorical and the emphasis is on the consequential aspect. The above verse also contains the basis for the saying, *the bitter end!*

Hebrews 4:12
*For the word of God is quick, and powerful, and sharper than any **two-edged sword**, piercing even to the dividing asunder of soul and spirit, and of the joints and marrow, and is a discerner of the thoughts and intents of the heart.*

Comment: The phrase 'let us hold fast our profession' two verses further on (v.14) is the key to what the chapter is about. The writer has dealt with unbelief (historically) and uses that to demonstrate how the present generation of Hebrews lose out by not entering into the good of the current rest available to them by relying on what the written Word of God says. He then goes on to explain the powerfulness of that word by stating that it is sharper than any two-edged sword in that it can cut right to the heart and test us in all matters. He uses the analogy of the soul and spirit, and bone and flesh, to illustrate the point.

The emphasis here is on the sharpness and penetrating effect of the (written) word of God. Besides going straight in it is capable of cutting both ways, convicting and converting some whilst condemning others. It is vastly different from the hedge trimmer that I use which, having teeth on both sides of the blade can only cut in one direction at a time!

God's word has far reaching effects for both saint and

sinner. It was instrumental in my salvation and, in case you don't know, that of every genuine convert. The application of it is meant to govern our lives. Thus, everything we believe and do should be tested against the Holy Scriptures.

Remember also that Ephesians 6:17 tells us that the sword of the Spirit is the written Word of God.

Read more about the effects of the Word of God in our next chapter dealing with the saying, *cut to the heart.*

Revelation 1:16
*And he had in his right hand seven stars: and out of his mouth went a sharp **two-edged sword**: and his countenance was as the sun shineth in his strength.*

Comment: The book of Revelation is full of symbols and the use of the phrase here is thus symbolical or, if you prefer, metaphorical. It appears early on in the Apostle John's introduction of the circumstances in which he comes to be writing — see chapter 1:9 — and the command to write of (1) those things which he had seen, (2) and the things which are, (3) and the things which shall be hereafter. Read the chapter for yourself. The many characteristics ascribed to the Lord Jesus Christ are equally important to our study.

The *sharp two-edged sword* phrase is descriptive of Christ's clinical (accurate) pronouncements detailed in chapters 2 and 3 concerning the seven churches in Asia Minor. The same truth is emphasised again in chapter 2:12. The emphasis in both references is on the Lord's absolute fitness to (righteously) judge the seven churches that come under his pronouncements. A different type of judgment comes later on in the Revelation.

Revelation 2:12
*And to the angel of the church in Pergamos write; These things saith he which hath the sharp **sword with two edges**;*

Comment: See above comments on Revelation 1:16.

In summary, we have identified the five verses containing our expression, examined the context to see what it means and see where the emphasis lies.

Chapter 40

Cut to the heart!

This has been a most difficult expression for which to get a satisfactory meaning, especially in the context of use in the Bible. Perhaps the best definition is: *absolute outrage at something said, or more usually, some truth hitting home*! It differs from other sayings such as 'the heart of the matter', 'cut right to the heart', 'cut to the core', and 'cut to the chase' etc.

Pardon the pun, but at the heart of this matter is a proper understanding as to which heart this expression refers. It is not the anatomical organ which is vital to human life. On the contrary, it is the centre of those hidden, emotional, intellectual and moral activities around which human beings live.

My personal check shows 841 occurrences of the word 'heart' in the Bible – more than enough for a thesis! You will be glad to know, however, that we confine our remarks here to the three occasions where it forms part of our expression. Actually, there are just two in the King James version of the Bible but, since the NKJV and some others substitute the word 'cut' for 'pricked' in Acts 2:37, we include that verse here also.

In the previous chapter we examined another expression, the five occurrences of it, its meaning and, in particular, where the emphasis seemed to lie. This time we examine what the phrase *cut to the heart* means and the different reactions that it brought! In fact, those reactions are either hinted at or clearly stated in the verses containing the very expression. The three verses are —

Acts 2:37
*Now when they heard this, they were **pricked in their heart**, and said unto Peter and to the rest of the apostles, Men and brethren, what shall we do?*

Acts 5:33
*When they heard that, they were **cut to the heart,** and took counsel to slay them.*

Acts 7:54
*When they heard these things, they were **cut to the heart,** and they gnashed on him with their teeth.*

In Acts 2 the Apostle Peter is addressing thousands of Jews on the day of Pentecost. His hearers had marvelled at the (120 plus) disciples' ability to speak in other known languages subsequent to the descent of the Holy Spirit. Most did not know what it all meant, while others mocked and suggested that the disciples were full of new wine (drunk).

Peter gave a comprehensive explanation, which included his accusing them of crucifying the Lord Jesus (a mere seven weeks earlier), how that God had raised Him from the dead, and how that He was now seated at God's right hand. Verse 37 then comes into play. Their conscience got the better of them; they sought advice as to what they should do and in verses 38-40 Peter gives the answer, 'Repent....' The result was positive and some 3,000 souls were converted. Take time to read the complete chapter for yourself at Appendix II.

The relevant part of Acts chapter 5 again involves Peter. Many miracles had been performed to the annoyance of the authorities; they were afraid of the spread of Christianity to their detriment. The apostles were imprisoned but miraculously escaped during the night. Found next day preaching in the temple, they were again arrested and brought before the council and high priest.

After the high priest vented his wrath upon them they answered, again accusing them of crucifying the Lord Jesus. They went on to explain that God had raised Him from the dead and that they (the disciples) were to preach repentance and forgiveness of sins. Verse 33 then comes into play.

One of the council, Gamaliel, interjected. He gave wise counsel to which everyone agreed, but the apostles were again beaten and threatened before being released. As has been seen, the net result of the preaching and witness of the apostles on this occasion was negative. Again, read the relevant part of the chapter for yourself at Appendix III

Acts chapter 7 (and part of Ch 6) concerns Stephen's preaching and his defence of the gospel. He is again arrested and brought before the council and, like Peter in Acts 2, gives a strong defence. Winding matters up, he accused his hearers of being stiff-necked, law breakers and murderers of, not only those who proclaimed the coming of the Just One (Lord Jesus), but of His very own death. Verse 54 then comes into play. They cast Stephen out of the city and stoned him to death. As with the Acts 5 situation, the outcome was negative. In both cases the hearers were so infuriated that they did not give way to reason. Again, read chapters 6 and 7 at Appendix IV.

The message was the same on all three occasions; it was pointed to the extent that it cut to the heart as already observed, but the outcomes differed! The parable of the soils in Matthew chapter 13 is a good illustration of this.

Jeremiah 17:9 reminds us that the heart is deceitful above all things, and desperately wicked. By nature it rejects that which is good. It is only the Spirit of God that can bring about a change.

In closing, not only can one harden their heart to the strivings of the Holy Spirit, but God, as in the case of Pharaoh (who hardened his own heart), can also harden the heart.

Chapter 41

Well able

This expression is a little problematic. In the biblical context it simply means: *to be more than capable of.* However, in everyday usage it is often used in a begrudging sense. For instance, one might say, "I can't understand why he is always getting a bus since he is well able to walk that short distance." Perhaps the phrase 'very able' might be more appropriate. Both expressions differ from yet another one, 'too able' which suggests the taking advantage of someone.

The *well able* expression is found only in Numbers 13:30. However, as we will see later, there are other verses where the sentiment could be fittingly applied. Numbers 13:30 reads —

*And Caleb stilled the people before Moses, and said, Let us go up at once, and possess it; for we are **well able** to overcome it.*

The children of Israel had been redeemed out of Egypt, reached Sinai, given the Law and set off on their journey to the Promised Land (Canaan) with Moses as their leader. They were guided by a pillar of cloud during the day and fire by night. After some months they reached Kadesh-Barnea and, whilst there, God instructed Moses to single out 12 men to go ahead and spy out the land to which they were journeying.

It is well known that two of them, Joshua and Caleb, brought back true reports while the others, false reports. Nevertheless, and against great opposition, Caleb made the statement in verse 30 that contains our expression. He was satisfied that they were more than capable of conquering the land. The expression lives on today.

Rather than unnecessarily going into all the detail surrounding the biblical use of the expression, I want to list three verses containing an 'able' phrase where the word 'well' could be added as a prefix. After all, our God is a mighty God. The verses need little comment —

Hebrews 7:25
*Wherefore he is **able also to save** them to the uttermost that come unto God by him, seeing he ever liveth to make intercession for them.*

2 Timothy 1:12
*...for I know whom I have believed, and am persuaded that he is **able to keep** that which I have committed unto him against that day.*

Matthew 10:28
And *fear not them which kill the body, but are not able to kill the soul: but rather fear him which is **able to destroy** both soul and body in hell.*

Chapter 42

A soft answer turneth away wrath

This expression is found in the book of Proverbs written by Solomon who, incidentally, also wrote Ecclesiastes, the Song of Solomon and two of the Psalms (72 and 127). Proverbs is the middle one of the five poetical books (Job, Psalms, Proverbs, Ecclesiastes, and Song of Solomon).

Sadly, Solomon did not practice all that he preached. As he got older he turned away from God. He had many wives, some of which followed other religions. With these, he broke the commandments by praying to other gods. The Bible says that Solomon's actions were evil (1 Kings 11:1-13). However, as we will see later in connection with another saying, it seems that he recovered somewhat, albeit with consequences. Despite his failings, the book of Proverbs is invaluable in that it still teaches wisdom to us today.

As stated in an earlier chapter, Solomon's proverbs do not start until chapter 10. Thereafter, they are divided into different sections. The first section — chapters 10 to 24 — deal mainly with the contrast between righteousness and wickedness and it is in this section that we get the verse containing our saying —

A soft answer turneth away wrath: but grievous words stir up anger. (Proverbs 15:1)

As stated elsewhere, the proverbs are mostly in the form of couplets. The two clauses of the couplet are generally related to each other by what has been termed parallelism. The verse in question is of the antithetic type in that the first clause is made stronger in the second clause by contrasting it with an opposite truth.

The verse in question, and hence, our saying, is a generality. There can be exceptions but that is not the point of focus here.

The phrase 'a soft answer turneth away wrath' needs little explanation other than to say that a gentle reply is unlikely to inflame the situation. However, a volatile situation may already exist and be the reason behind any confrontation as inferred by the word 'answer'. In those circumstances a soft or gentle reply may well prevent a further inflaming of the situation. A calm demeanour may also go a long way in achieving the same results. On the other hand, no answer at all may have the opposite effect!

Of course, gentleness of speech, whether or not in reply to a question, is generally the preferred choice.

The principle of the proverb applies across the board whether or not one is a Christian. The greatest example of them all is the Lord Jesus Christ. In addition, we have the written word of God in its entirety. Unsurprisingly, one does not have to go outside Proverbs 15 to see the same principle reinforced in other verses such as 2, 4, 7, 18 etc, or obtain good advice for godly living. Take time to read the chapter and note those proverbs which apply to the tongue, eyes, mind, lips, heart, thoughts, ear, soul etc.

Chapter 43

A word in season

If you read Proverbs 15 as exhorted to in the previous chapter you may have noticed another everyday saying in verse 23 —

*A man hath joy by the answer of his mouth: and **a word** spoken **in** due **season**, how good is it!*

The same expression is found in Isaiah 50:4 —

*The Lord God hath given me the tongue of the learned, that I should know how to speak **a word in season** to him that is weary: he wakeneth morning by morning, he wakeneth mine ear to hear as the learned.*

Solomon is the speaker in Proverbs 15, and the coming Messiah in Isaiah 50:4. The application of Christ's words, in the context, were for the weary exiles but later on in Matthew's Gospel He could throw out the great invitation, *'Come unto me, all ye that labour and are heavy laden and I will give you rest.'* (Matthew 11:28)

In short, the expression simply means saying the right thing at the right time and, as the latter verse indicates, it is usually in circumstances where someone needs advice or encouragement. I say usually, because in some cases it needs to be a word of admonishment.

In a previous chapter we referred to Job's so-called comforters. Their onslaught against Job was most certainly not a word in season. By contrast, the Lord Jesus never spoke an idle word. John 7:46 states, *'Never man spake like this man.'*

Central to the expression is its timing, and what it is that is said. It may be a word of encouragement, advice, or perhaps, admonishment at a critical time. It might not be a solution for life, but, rather, for the immediate future. It could be brought by the Thought for Today programme that you hear on the radio, a verse in a daily readings calendar, or a verse on a Get Well card. Of course, it does not even need to be along spiritual lines! Furthermore, what is said, although taken completely out of context, could be the very thing that achieves the desired result.

To illustrate the latter point, consider the number of verses in Scripture which are not so-called 'gospel verses' yet have been instrumental in a person's salvation. Genesis 6:3 *(My spirit shall not always strive with man),* Mark 8:36 *(For what shall it profit a man...),* Revelation 3:20 *(Behold I stand at the door and knock...)* are but a few examples.

There are numerous examples of 'a word in season' in the Bible. Read the account of the woman taken in adultery in John 8:1-11. Note verses 7 and 9 in particular! Read the account of the apostles' second persecution in Acts 5:12-40 (which we studied earlier in connection with the 'cut to the heart' saying). Note the intervention of Gamaliel in verses 33-39. If you are a young person and enjoy a good adventure story then turn to Acts chapter 27 for the account of Paul's voyage (and shipwreck) to Rome. In particular, note verses 20-25 and 33-36. You can identify others for yourself.

Pardon another personal reference which illustrates the point. For some reason or other I was under great pressure as I travelled to work almost 35 years ago. However, I was playing a tape of gospel music. (I had played it often before.) The hymn being sung was, *What a Friend we have in Jesus.* After a couple of verses the singer stopped, recited a few lines which included the words *take it to the Lord in prayer,* and then said, 'The problem is that we take our burden to the Lord, but then bring it away again.' He stated emphatically, 'Take it to the Lord AND LEAVE IT THERE.' I heard those words as never before. What a tonic! Was that not a word in season?

Almost as an aside, but here is a word of warning to those people who get encouragement from a verse and then attempt to force it down another's throat expecting them to get the same blessing. Experience shows that things seldom work that way. The recipient must see things for themselves. Reverently speaking, this is where the work of the Holy Spirit comes in.

A word in season transcends all boundaries – giver and recipient alike. And, as suggested earlier, it need not have a spiritual connotation. There is, however, a massive resource available to those who can apply them wisely, in the shape of the Holy Bible. 2 Timothy 3:16 states —

All scripture is given by inspiration of God, and is profitable for doctrine, for reproof, for correction, for instruction in righteousness: That the man of God may be perfect, thoroughly furnished unto all good works.

Summarised, this verse tells us —

What is right,
What is not right,
How to get right, *and*
How to stay right!

Chapter 44

The sun shines on the righteous

Back in Chapter 42 we indicated that the first group of Solomon's proverbs (Chs 10-24), deal mainly with the contrast between righteousness and wickedness. As we examine the present saying we shall see some more of these contrasts.

The exact phrase, 'The sun shines on the righteous' is not found in the Bible. However, there are many verses to support it and some of these will feature later.

The expression infers that the sun shines <u>only</u> on the righteous and this has often become a talking point. Upon hearing it quoted some facetiously suggest that the sun surely shines on everyone. They know full well that the person is speaking metaphorically, while they themselves are speaking of things literally!

Some mistakenly link the saying to the latter half of Matthew 5:45 (part of the Sermon on the Mount) – *For He maketh His sun to rise on the evil and on the good, and sendeth rain on the just and on the unjust.* They take no account of the fact that the sun also shines on those who are not righteous, and that the rain also falls on everyone.

Psalm 97:11 is a better verse in support – *'Light is sown for the righteous, and gladness for the upright in heart.'* The New Living Translation is more easily understood – *Light shines on the godly, and joy on those whose hearts are right.'* The Psalmist is speaking of the end times and, more precisely, the Day of the Lord, when Christ returns to earth to judge sin and vindicate His chosen earthly people. That vindication will be seen by everyone, just like the bright, bright light of a sunrise!

The Psalmist recognises that God's chosen earthly people are going through dark times but gives hope there will be 'light at the end of tunnel' when the Lord Jesus rules in righteousness, with His people then basking in the sunshine of His favour. It is no surprise that in those days the Saviour has the title, 'Sun of Righteousness' ascribed to Him (Malachi 4:2). Of course, one does not have to wait until the end times to experience God's favour.

Before saying more about the expression we make one further comment regarding the end times. In Matthew chapter 13 the Lord Jesus gave six kingdom parables (there are eight parables in total in the chapter). Verses 24-30 deal with the parable of the tares and verses 36-43 record the Lord's interpreting of it privately later on to His disciples. He concludes by saying – *'Then shall the righteous shine forth as the sun in the kingdom of their Father....'* Have you noticed how the words 'sun' and 'righteous' have been switched around? Please take a moment to ponder the significance of this.

To be righteous means to be morally justified, or as Psalm 97:11 suggests, upright (in heart). Thus the expression *the sun shines on the righteous* means that the favour of God is upon the upright. This does not mean that such people will be exempt from all sorts of trials. Take Job for example; he was 'perfect and upright' yet went through the severest of trials by losing wealth, health and family — all on the same day!

The word 'righteous' is found 256 times in the Bible. Derivatives of it appear another 320 times. In fact, the word, in one form of another, is found in 75% of the Bible books and that surely is a study in itself!

In closing, we list a sample of verses which, either, support the veracity of our saying, contrast the blessings of righteousness to the consequences of wickedness, or encourage God's people in their time of trial —

Exodus 20:5-6 (Number 3 of the Ten Commandments)
Thou shalt not bow down thyself to them, nor serve them: for I the Lord thy God am a jealous God, visiting the iniquity of the fathers upon the children unto the third and fourth generation of them that hate me; And shewing mercy unto thousands of them that love me, and keep my commandments.

Psalm 34:15 (& 1 Peter 3:12)
The eyes of the Lord are upon the righteous, and his ears are
open unto their cry.

Psalm 34:16
The face of the Lord is against them that do evil...

Psalm 34:17
*The righteous cry and the Lord heareth, and delivereth them
out of all their troubles.*

Psalm 34:18
*The Lord is nigh unto them that are of a broken heart; and
saveth such as be of a contrite spirit.*

Psalm 34:19
*Many are the afflictions of the righteous: but the Lord
delivereth him out of them all.*

Psalm 37:39-40
*But the salvation of the righteous is of the Lord: he is their
strength in the time of trouble.
And the Lord shall help them, and deliver them: he shall
deliver them from the wicked, and save them, because they
trust in him.*

Matthew 25:46
And these (professors, rather than possessors) *shall go away
into everlasting punishment: but the righteous into life eternal.*

Chapter 45

Set your (own) house in order

The inclusion of the bracketed word 'own' in the above phrase shows that there are two closely related sayings. The first, *set your house in order*, has no distasteful connotation whereas the second, *set your <u>own</u> house in order*, is normally said as a rebuke! Both are generally used metaphorically, albeit after the fashion of a literal tidying up of a house.

The first of these two sayings refers to the arranging or settling of one's affairs, especially in light of some forthcoming event. The second calls for the correction of one's own behaviour before criticising others for the same thing. In many ways it is similar to the proverb of 'taking the beam out of your own eye before trying to take the mote out of someone else's eye' as found in Matthew 7:5.

For the purposes of this study we concentrate on the first of the two sayings.

There are essentially three verses in the Bible which contain our saying. Two are virtually identical – 2 Kings 20:1 and Isaiah 38:1. They read —

In those days was Hezekiah sick unto death. And the prophet Isaiah the son of Amoz came to him, and said unto him, Thus saith the Lord, **Set thine house in order***; for thou shalt die, and not live.*

The third verse, which has sad consequences, is 2 Samuel 17:23 and reads —

And when Ahithophel saw that his counsel was not followed, he saddled his ass, and arose, and gat him home to his house, to his city, and **put his household in order,** *and hanged himself, and died, and was buried in the sepulchre of his father.*

For the purposes of this short chapter we concentrate only on the story of Hezekiah.

Along with the rapture of the church there is no more important event for which one needs to prepare than that of death. This was the case as regards Hezekiah and the message he received through the prophet Isaiah. Everyone knows that death comes sooner or later, but to be confronted with it unexpectedly is quite a shock. This frequently comes as a result of the diagnosis of a serious medical condition or an accident.

If one reads the entire narrative they will discover how Hezekiah prayed for an 'extension' of life and that he was granted another 15 years! In one sense it was the worst thing that could have happened since three years later his son Manasseh was born and went on to become the most evil king that ever reigned over Israel (2 Chronicles 33:9). On the other hand, it had to happen considering that Manasseh is in the royal line of our blessed Saviour. See Matthew 1:1-17 and verse 10 in particular.

All reasonable people set their house in order by making plans for the future. These often include arrangements for education, holidays, marriage, honeymoon, a home, children, savings plans, funeral arrangements, and in some cases funeral plans (with advance payment). Arrangements have to be made, tickets obtained, etc. Sadly, when it comes to spiritual matters there is not the same level of preparation.

While much counsel can be directed towards those who are not saved, the aims of the saying can also be applied to those who are. For instance, all believers need to be reminded that they have to face the Judgment Seat of Christ (for reward; not punishment). Also, there may be that long running sore where relationships have broken down and forgiveness has not been offered with a view to reconciliation. (Just think of the number of occasions that you have heard of a death and wished you had done something before the person had died. But, alas, the opportunity has gone!)

Turning to the 'thou shalt die, and not live' element of the verse, there are instances of an opposite statement in

Scripture. For example, in Psalm 118:17 the writer states, ' I shall not die, but live' (and declare the works of the Lord). That verse became very precious over 20 years ago to a friend of mine as he lay on a hospital bed with serious injuries sustained in a vicious assault.

Then, with another twist, there is Job, whose plight we have addressed elsewhere in this book. He asked, *'If a man die, shall he live again?'* (Job 14:14) Thankfully, that question was answered by the Lord Jesus in John 11:25-26 - *'I am the resurrection, and the life: he that believeth in me, though he were dead, yet shall he live: And whosoever liveth and believeth in me shall never die. Believest thou this?'*

Going still further, Job, in his predicament, wished that he had never been conceived, never mind born. He even wished that he had died at birth! There are some parallels between him and Jonah who asked God to take his life from him since he considered it would be better for him to die rather than live!

In sharp contrast, the apostle Paul could say, *'For to me to live is Christ, and to die is gain.'* (Philippians 1:21), or, as St. Patrick translated it, *'For me to live is Christ, and to die is more of Christ!'* A few years later the same Paul could say, *'I am now ready to be offered, and the time of my departure is at hand. I have fought a good fight, I have finished my course, I have kept the faith.'* (2 Timothy 4:6-7) What an example he set us!

In conclusion, here are some verses to suggest the importance of setting your house in order —

Hebrews 9:27
It is appointed unto men once to die, but after this the judgment.

Mark 8:36
For what shall it profit a man, if he shall gain the whole world, and lose his own soul?'

2 Corinthians 6:2:
Behold, now is the accepted time; behold, now is the day of salvation.

Proverbs 27:1
Boast not thyself of tomorrow; for thou knowest not what a day may bring forth.

Genesis 6:3
My spirit shall not always strive with man.

1 Samuel 20:3
...there is but a step between me and death.

Chapter 46

A red sky at night is a shepherd's delight; a red sky in the morning is a shepherd's warning!

This saying is found only in Matthew's Gospel. However, the occasion on which it was spoken by the Lord Jesus is also recorded in Mark 8:10-13. Matthew 16:2-3 reads —

He answered and said unto them, When it is evening, ye say, It will be fair weather: for the sky is red. And in the morning, It will be foul weather today: for the sky is red and lowering. O ye hypocrites, ye can discern the face of the sky; but can ye not discern the signs of the times?

On a another occasion, but in the same context, the Lord Jesus expressed similar sentiments when He stated —

When ye see a cloud rise out of the west, straightway ye say, There cometh a shower; and so it is. And when ye see the south wind blow, ye say, There will be heat; and it cometh to pass. Ye hypocrites, ye can discern the face of the sky and of the earth; but how is it that ye do not discern this time? (Luke 12:54-56)

There is some interesting information on the Met Office webpage in regard to this saying which I reproduce here with permission —

Red sky at night and other weather sayings
In the days before weather forecasts, people often turned to sayings and proverbs to provide an indication of what tomorrow's weather might bring. In this article we look at some of these sayings and whether there is any science behind the saying.

Dating back thousands of years, weather forecasting had to rely less on scientific data and more on human experience. From this, developed the old weather sayings and phrases we see and hear today. The sayings became particularly important in sailing and agriculture as they looked for reliable forecasts ahead.

Sky at night
The concept of "Red sky at night, shepherd's delight. Red sky in the morning, shepherd's warning" first appears in the Bible in the Gospel of Matthew. It is an old weather saying often used at sunrise and sunset to signify the changing sky and originally known to help the shepherds prepare for the next day's weather. Despite there being global variations in this saying such as "Red sky at night, sailors delight. Red sky in morning, sailors warning", the scientific understanding behind such occurrences remains the same.

Why does red sky appear at sunrise and sunset?
The saying is most reliable when weather systems predominantly come from the west as they do in the UK. "Red sky at night, shepherds delight" can often be proven true, since red sky at night means fair weather is generally headed towards you.

A red sky appears when dust and small particles are trapped in the atmosphere by high pressure. This scatters blue light and leaving only red light to give the sky its notable appearance.

A red sky at sunset means high pressure is moving in from the west so therefore the next day will usually be dry and pleasant. "Red sky in the morning, shepherds warning" means a red sky appears due to the high pressure weather system having already moved east meaning the good weather has passed, most likely making way for a wet and windy low pressure system.

Contains public sector information licensed under the Open Government Licence v1.0 www.metoffice.gov.uk/learning/learn-about-the-weather/how- weather-works/red-sky-at-night [2/5/16]

The tell-tale signs for forecasting the weather as related by the Lord Jesus in Matthew 16 were contained in His rebuff of the

Pharisees and Sadducees' demand for a sign from heaven. With sufficient explanation having been given as to the meaning of the expression we develop the context of its use in our next chapter.

Chapter 47

Sign(s) of the times

This chapter should be read in conjunction with Chapter 46.

As previously stated, the *red sky at night* saying is contained in the opening verses of Matthew chapter 16. So, too, is the current saying.

Chapter 16 is extremely significant. It confirms the turning point in the offer of the kingdom of Heaven to the Jew, contains the great confession of Peter that Christ is the Son of the Living God (v.16), makes mention of the (universal) church for the first time (v.18) and contains the first of multiple disclosures by Christ to His disciples regarding His imminent journey to Jerusalem, His death, burial and resurrection (v.21).

Returning to the opening verses of the chapter (Matthew Ch 16) for the context of our saying, the Pharisees and the Sadducees set aside their religious differences and came together in an attempt to trip up the Lord Jesus. They demanded a sign from Heaven as to His divinity and mission notwithstanding they had just witnessed the feeding of the 4,000+ (in the previous chapter), and lots more besides. The only sign that the Lord Jesus promised was that of the prophet Jonah. That surely was the greatest sign – it was from Heaven, and followed within a few months. Christ's yielding up of His spirit and His subsequent resurrection is central to the Christian faith (1 Corinthians 15:1-17).

It is best to quote Matthew 16 verses 2-4 here —

*He answered and said unto them, When it is evening, ye say, It will be fair weather: for the sky is red. And in the morning, It will be foul weather to day: for the sky is red and lowering. O ye hypocrites, ye can discern the face of the sky; but can ye not discern the **signs of the times**? A wicked and adulterous generation seeketh after a sign; and there shall no* *sign be given unto it, but the sign of the prophet Jonas. And he left them, and departed.*

Mark 8:12 adds that the Lord Jesus sighed deeply in spirit. He said what He did, and with great feeling.

The sign of Jonah was that of Christ's death, burial and resurrection on the third day. The concluding phrase, 'And he left them and departed' was a clear act of judgment upon them.

The 'signs of the times' referred to by the Lord Jesus in verse 3 obviously refer to the times immediately prior to, and including the early part of His public ministry. They include the departure of the sceptre from Judah, the ministry of John the Baptist, the arrival of their Messiah, His mighty words and works, the evil that existed, etc. The concluding part of Luke 12:56 uses the term, *'this time'*.

The inability of the Pharisees and Sadducees to discern the signs of the times obviously refers to their spiritual discernment.

I am always reminded of our expression every time I travel along a certain road where someone imaginatively advertises their business by displaying a small sign that reads, *The Signs of the Times.* There are, of course, other businesses, websites, books, films etc similarly named.

The Cambridge Advanced Learner's Dictionary & Thesaurus defines the phrase as: *Something that is typical of the (bad) way things are now* and goes on to give the example – *These riots are a sign of the times.* Note well how they have bracketed the word 'bad'. Generally speaking, the expression is only used to describe worsening conditions.

There are many signs of the times to be observed in the Bible, especially those relating to the 'end times'. The latter expression describes events that have yet to take place, especially those in the run up to the 'end of the age'. (See next chapter.)

Notable end time verses include —

Daniel 12:4
... even to the time of the end: many shall run to and fro, and knowledge shall be increased.

Matthew 24:4-5, 11

... many shall come in My Name, saying, I am Christ ... and many false prophets shall arise and deceive many.

Matthew 24:32-33
Now learn a parable of the fig tree; When his branch is yet tender, and putteth forth leaves, ye know that summer is nigh: So likewise ye, when ye shall see all these things (mentioned in the preceding verses) *know that it is near, even at the doors.*

Matthew 24:37
... But as the days of Noah were (refusal to listen to the warnings) *so shall also the coming of the Son of man be.*

Luke 21:25-26
... and upon the earth distress of nations, with perplexity; the sea and the waves roaring; Men's hearts failing them for fear, and for looking after those things which are coming on the earth: for the powers of heaven shall be shaken.

2 Thessalonians 2:3
... Let no man deceive you by any means: for that day shall not come, except there come a falling away first, and that man of sin be revealed, the son of perdition.

1 Timothy 4:1
... Now the Spirit speaketh expressly, that in the latter times some shall depart from the faith, giving heed to seducing spirits, and doctrines of devils.

2 Timothy 4:3-4
... For the time will come when they will not endure sound doctrine; but after their own lusts shall they heap to themselves teachers, having itching ears; And they shall turn away their ears from the truth, and shall be turned unto fables.

Chapter 48

It's not the end of the world!

The Cambridge Advanced Learner's Dictionary & Thesaurus defines the phrase as: *If something is not the end of the world, it will not cause very serious problems* and goes on to give the example – *I'm really hoping to win, but it won't be the end of the world if I don't.* A synonym is: *don't make a mountain out of a molehill.*

Occasionally the phrase is reversed, e.g., someone who sees no way out of a disastrous situation might be tempted to think that it *was the end of the world!*

The phrase *end of the world* is found seven times in the Bible. (There are other occasions when a slightly different form of words suggests the same thing.) In the first two — Psalms 19:4 and Isaiah 62:11 — the meaning relates to the extent, e.g., the uttermost parts of the earth. On the other five occasions the emphasis is on the timing.

As is sometimes the case, the word 'world' is an unfortunate translation. A better translation is 'age'. Generally speaking, this term refers to the time at the end of the Great Tribulation when Christ comes back in His Second Advent. At least one exception to this is Hebrews 9:26. The verse reads —

*For then must he often have suffered since the foundation of the world: but now once in **the end of the world** hath he appeared to put away sin by the sacrifice of himself.*

The context here makes it clear that this refers to the period following the failed Jewish economy when Christ came into world and was, as we now know, at least 2,000 years earlier than the era to which it generally refers.

The four remaining Scriptures containing the phrase under discussion are —

Matthew 13:39-40 (Occasion: Christ's delivery of the earlier kingdom parables) —

*The enemy that sowed them is the devil; the harvest is **the end of the world;** and the reapers are the angels. As therefore the tares are gathered and burned in the fire; so shall it be in **the end of this world.***

Matthew 13:49-50 (Occasion: Christ's delivery of the earlier kingdom parables) —

*So shall it be at **the end of the world:** the angels shall come forth, and sever the wicked from among the just, And shall cast them into the furnace of fire: there shall be wailing and gnashing of teeth.*

Matthew 24:3 (Occasion: The Olivet Discourse) —

*And as he sat upon the Mount of Olives, the disciples came unto him privately, saying, Tell us, when shall these things be? And what shall be the sign of thy coming, and of **the end of the world?***

Matthew 28:19-20 (Occasion: The Great Commission just prior to the Lord's ascension) —

*Go ye therefore, and teach all nations, baptising them in the name of the Father, and of the Son, and of the Holy Ghost: Teaching them to observe all things whatsoever I have commanded you: and, lo, I am with you alway, even unto **the end of the world.** Amen.*

The real end of the world, as we know it, does not take place until after the Millennium when we enter into the Eternal State with a new Heaven and a new Earth! (Revelation 21:1-22:5)

Chapter 49

In the twinkling of an eye

From 0 to 60 (mph) in 4 seconds is exceptionally fast for any motorcar. Two shakes of a lamb's tail is even faster. But fastest of all is the twinkling of an eye — even faster than the batting of an eyelid!

One dictionary defines 'twinkling' as: *the time that it takes to blink once.* Another defines it as: *an instant; very quickly.* Synonyms of it include: *in a second, in a minute, in a moment, in a trice, in a flash, in an instant, in no time at all, before you know it.*

The expression is found only once in the Authorised Version of the Bible (1 Corinthians 15:52) and the verse reads —

*In a moment, **in the twinkling of an eye**, at the last trump: for the trumpet shall sound, and the dead shall be raised incorruptible, and we shall be changed.*

The observant will have noticed that the phrase 'in the twinkling of an eye' is preceded by the synonym *in a moment.* The terms reinforce each other. Although only used once in the Bible, the expression 'in the twinkling of an eye' was apparently used frequently in Jewish writings to signify how speedily and suddenly something is done.

The verse in which our saying is contained is part of the greatest resurrection chapter of our Bible (1 Corinthians 15); the latter part of which should be read in conjunction with 1 Thessalonians 4:13-18 which deals with the rapture of the church. Of necessity, the resurrection of all believers who die during the church age, and the rapture of the church, are an integral part of the same blessed event.

While there are a number of resurrections mentioned in Scripture there is none more important than that of our Lord Jesus, who, in 1 Corinthians chapter 15, is described as 'Christ the firstfruits'. Some verses earlier it states, *And if Christ be not risen, then is our preaching vain, and your faith is also vain* (v.13) and, *If Christ be not raised, your faith is vain; ye are yet in your sins* (v.17). These are fundamental truths for the believer.

As inferred earlier, 1 Corinthians 15:51-53 and 1 Thessalonians 4:13-18 are the two classic portions of Scripture that describe the resurrection and rapture. The Thessalonian passage tells us, *"For the Lord Himself shall descend from heaven with a shout ...and the dead in Christ shall rise first: then we which are alive and remain shall be caught up together with them in the clouds, to meet the Lord in the air: and so shall we ever be with the Lord."*

1 Corinthians 15:51-53 describes the briefness of this event and details what happens at that precise moment — *"We shall not all sleep, but we shall all be changed, In a moment, **in the twinkling of an eye**, ...the dead shall be raised incorruptible, and we shall be changed. For this corruptible must put on incorruption, and this mortal must put on immortality."*

By reading these two complementary passages we see that it is the dead in Christ, i.e., the saved of the church age, which are raised first. In the briefest of moments which we have been considering they will be given a new body that will never again be subject to corruption, rot or decay. It matters not whether the believer has just died, been dead for months, years, or even hundreds of years; or whether their body has been interred, cremated, lost at sea, or whatever.

As part of the same event those who are saved and still alive will have their body changed to one that will never die. And all this will happen *in the twinkling of an eye*. It is at that very moment that the grave will give way to victory, and death for the believer will have lost its sting. In other words, graves or whatever will deliver up the bodies of those believers who sleep, and believers who are living at that moment will never die. This great truth is embodied in the words of the Lord Jesus Himself when He said, *"I am the resurrection, and the life: he that believeth in me, though he were dead, yet shall he live: And whosoever liveth and believeth in me shall never die."* (John 11:25, 26).

The resurrection that we have been studying is part of that category which is unto life. This is clear from the verse just quoted and other verses such as John 5:29. The 'dead in Christ' (only) phrase in 1 Thessalonians 4:16 infers there must be another resurrection. John 5:25-29 and Revelation 20:11-15 make it abundantly clear that there is, and, in contrast to the first resurrection (by both type and order), this is called the resurrection of damnation (John 5:29).

Believers should note that "we shall all (believers both dead and living) be changed" (v.51). The Puritan commentator, John Gill, observes: "the change upon the bodies of living saints will be so quick, that it will be done in a trice, before a man can shut his eyes and open them again; so that it will be as it were imperceptible, and without the least sensation of pain". What a lovely thought!

No parallel description is given of the wicked dead who are the second resurrection. It will not take place for at least 1,007 years — perhaps a little longer — after the first, and no one should want to be part of it.

Chapter 50

No rest for the wicked

The sentiments of this saying can be found over and over again in Scripture. As with some of the previous sayings, we do not get the exact phrase but, rather, the basis for it. However, Isaiah 57:20-21 comes close. The verse reads —

*But **the wicked** are like the troubled sea, when it **cannot rest,** whose waters cast up mire and dirt. (v.20)*
There is no peace, saith my God, to the wicked.(v.21)

Verse 21 is essentially a repeat of an earlier verse, Isaiah 48:22. The verses in question are a throwback to disobedient Israel.

The absence of rest is seen as punishment. To some extent the same truth applies today but will be manifested in a fuller way in a coming day. Israel's past, present and future have been touched upon in other chapters and need not be further commented upon here.

When thinking of the *no rest for the wicked* expression in the context of the teachings of Scripture it is clear that the wicked neither deserve nor get rest. Today, however, we stray somewhat and, while still applying the expression literally, use it to describe good or hardworking people who have extra work brought upon them, whether of their own volition or not. They use it with tongue-in-cheek to suggest their workload is a result of present or past wickedness!

Christians have faults (and many of them), but by way of contrast it is lovely to think how that the favour of God is upon them, both in time and eternity! We touched on these truths in chapter 44 when dealing with the saying, *the sun shines on the righteous.*

An adapted version of the hymn *Count your blessings*.
(See Chapter 25)

When you're on the pension

When you're on the pension and your friends are few,
Don't sit down and worry like the others do,
Think of all the blessings of the welfare state,
Everything is planned for you— so do not wait!

Refrain
Count your blessings name them one by one,
Count your blessings name them two by two, three
Count your blessings name them by the score,
And it will surprise you there are millions more.

Are you hard of hearing do your friends all shout?
Do they talk in whispers that you can't make out?
It's time for an appointment— to the clinic go,
And you'll get a hearing aid to cure your woe!

When you go out walking to your favourite store,
Do your feet start aching and get very sore?
Go to your chiropodist for he'll make them right,
Set the music playing, and you'll dance all night!

Have your eyes got weaker, so you cannot see?
Colours seem more faded than they used to be!
Get yourself a pair of specs, they'll look just fine,
And your day will brighten and the sun will shine!

Have you got the toothache, are your teeth all bad?
When you look into the mirror are you sad?
Go and see the dentist— in a little while,
He'll fix you up with dentures and you'll smile, smile, smile!

Appendix II

Acts 2 v 1-47 (Read in conjunction with Chapter 40)

1 And when the day of Pentecost was fully come, they were all with one accord in one place.

2 And suddenly there came a sound from heaven as of a rushing mighty wind, and it filled all the house where they were sitting.

3 And there appeared unto them cloven tongues like as of fire, and it sat upon each of them.

4 And they were all filled with the Holy Ghost, and began to speak with other tongues, as the Spirit gave them utterance.

5 And there were dwelling at Jerusalem Jews, devout men, out of every nation under heaven.

6 Now when this was noised abroad, the multitude came together, and were confounded, because that every man heard them speak in his own language.

7 And they were all amazed and marvelled, saying one to another, Behold, are not all these which speak Galilaeans?

8 And how hear we every man in our own tongue, wherein we were born?

9 Parthians, and Medes, and Elamites, and the dwellers in Mesopotamia, and in Judaea, and Cappadocia, in Pontus, and Asia,

10 Phrygia, and Pamphylia, in Egypt, and in the parts of Libya about Cyrene, and strangers of Rome, Jews and proselytes,

11 Cretes and Arabians, we do hear them speak in our tongues the wonderful works of God.

12 And they were all amazed, and were in doubt, saying one to another, What meaneth this?

13 Others mocking said, These men are full of new wine.

14 But Peter, standing up with the eleven, lifted up hisvoice, and said unto them, Ye men of Judaea, and all ye that dwell atJerusalem, be this known unto you, and hearken to my words:

15 For these are not drunken, as ye suppose, seeing it is but the third hour of the day.

16 But this is that which was spoken by the prophet Joel;

17 And it shall come to pass in the last days, saith God, I will pour out of my Spirit upon all flesh: and your sons and your daughters shall prophesy, and your young men shall see visions, and your old men shall dream dreams:

18 And on my servants and on my handmaidens I will pour out in those days of my Spirit; and they shall prophesy:

19 And I will shew wonders in heaven above, and signs in the earth beneath; blood, and fire, and vapour of smoke:

20 The sun shall be turned into darkness, and the moon into blood, before that great and notable day of the Lord come:

21 And it shall come to pass, that whosoever shall call on the name of the Lord shall be saved.

22 Ye men of Israel, hear these words; Jesus of Nazareth, a man approved of God among you by miracles and wonders and signs, which God did by him in the midst of you, as ye yourselves also know:

23 Him, being delivered by the determinate counsel and foreknowledge of God, ye have taken, and by wicked hands have crucified and slain:

24 Whom God hath raised up, having loosed the pains of death: because it was not possible that he should be holden of it.

25 For David speaketh concerning him, I foresaw the Lord always before my face, for he is on my right hand, that I should not be moved:

26 Therefore did my heart rejoice, and my tongue was glad; moreover also my flesh shall rest in hope:

27 Because thou wilt not leave my soul in hell, neither wilt thou suffer thine Holy One to see corruption.

28 Thou hast made known to me the ways of life; thou shalt make me full of joy with thy countenance.

29 Men and brethren, let me freely speak unto you of the patriarch David, that he is both dead and buried, and his sepulchre is with us unto this day.

30 Therefore being a prophet, and knowing that God had sworn with an oath to him, that of the fruit of his loins, according to the flesh, he would raise up Christ to sit on his throne;

31 He seeing this before spake of the resurrection of Christ, that his soul was not left in hell, neither his flesh did see corruption.

32 This Jesus hath God raised up, whereof we all are witnesses.

33 Therefore being by the right hand of God exalted, and having received of the Father the promise of the Holy Ghost, he hath shed forth this, which ye now see and hear.

34 For David is not ascended into the heavens: but he saith himself, The LORD said unto my Lord, Sit thou on my right hand,

35 Until I make thy foes thy footstool.

36 Therefore let all the house of Israel know assuredly, that God hath made that same Jesus, whom ye have crucified, both Lord and Christ.

37 Now when they heard this, they were pricked in their heart, and said unto Peter and to the rest of the apostles, Men and brethren, what shall we do?

38 Then Peter said unto them, Repent, and be baptized every one of you in the name of Jesus Christ for the remission of sins, and ye shall receive the gift of the Holy Ghost.

39 For the promise is unto you, and to your children, and to all that are afar off, even as many as the Lord our God shall call.

40 And with many other words did he testify and exhort, saying, Save yourselves from this untoward generation.

41 Then they that gladly received his word were baptized: and the same day there were added unto them about three thousand souls.

42 And they continued stedfastly in the apostles' doctrine and fellowship, and in breaking of bread, and in prayers.

43 And fear came upon every soul: and many wonders and signs were done by the apostles.

44 And all that believed were together, and had all things common;

45 And sold their possessions and goods, and parted them to all men, as every man had need.

46 And they, continuing daily with one accord in the temple, and breaking bread from house to house, did eat their meat with gladness and singleness of heart,

47 Praising God, and having favour with all the people. And the Lord added to the church daily such as should be saved.

Appendix III

Acts 5 v 12-42 (Read in conjunction with Chapter 40)

12 And by the hands of the apostles were many signs and wonders wrought among the people; (and they were all with one accord in Solomon's porch.

13 And of the rest durst no man join himself to them: but the people magnified them.

14 And believers were the more added to the Lord, multitudes both of men and women.)

15 Insomuch that they brought forth the sick into the streets, and laid them on beds and couches, that at the least the shadow of Peter passing by might overshadow some of them.

16 There came also a multitude out of the cities round about unto Jerusalem, bringing sick folks, and them which were vexed with unclean spirits: and they were healed every one.

17 Then the high priest rose up, and all they that were with him, (which is the sect of the Sadducees,) and were filled with indignation,

18 And laid their hands on the apostles, and put them in the common prison.

19 But the angel of the Lord by night opened the prison doors, and brought them forth, and said,

20 Go, stand and speak in the temple to the people all the words of this life.

21 And when they heard that, they entered into the temple early in the morning, and taught. But the high priest came, and they that were with him, and called the council together, and all the senate of the children of Israel, and sent to the prison to have them brought.

22 But when the officers came, and found them not in the prison, they returned, and told,

23 Saying, The prison truly found we shut with all safety, and the keepers standing without before the doors: but when we had opened, we found no man within.

24 Now when the high priest and the captain of the temple and the

chief priests heard these things, they doubted of them whereunto this would grow.

25 Then came one and told them, saying, Behold, the men whom ye put in prison are standing in the temple, and teaching the people.

26 Then went the captain with the officers, and brought them without violence: for they feared the people, lest they should have been stoned.

27 And when they had brought them, they set them before the council: and the high priest asked them,

28 Saying, Did not we straitly command you that ye should not teach in this name? and, behold, ye have filled Jerusalem with your doctrine, and intend to bring this man's blood upon us.

29 Then Peter and the other apostles answered and said, We ought to obey God rather than men.

30 The God of our fathers raised up Jesus, whom ye slew and hanged on a tree.

31 Him hath God exalted with his right hand to be a Prince and a Saviour, for to give repentance to Israel, and forgiveness of sins.

32 And we are his witnesses of these things; and so is also the Holy Ghost, whom God hath given to them that obey him.

33 When they heard that, they were cut to the heart, and took counsel to slay them.

34 Then stood there up one in the council, a Pharisee, named Gamaliel, a doctor of the law, had in reputation among all the people, and commanded to put the apostles forth a little space;

35 And said unto them, Ye men of Israel, take heed to yourselves what ye intend to do as touching these men.

36 For before these days rose up Theudas, boasting himself to be somebody; to whom a number of men, about four hundred, joined themselves: who was slain; and all, as many as obeyed him, were scattered, and brought to nought.

37 After this man rose up Judas of Galilee in the days of the taxing, and drew away much people after him: he also perished; and all, even as many as obeyed him, were dispersed.

38 And now I say unto you, Refrain from these men, and let them alone: for if this counsel or this work be of men, it will come to nought:

39 But if it be of God, ye cannot overthrow it; lest haply ye be found even to fight against God.

40 And to him they agreed: and when they had called the apostles, and beaten them, they commanded that they should not speak in the name of Jesus, and let them go.

41 And they departed from the presence of the council, rejoicing that they were counted worthy to suffer shame for his name.

42 And daily in the temple, and in every house, they ceased not to teach and preach Jesus Christ.

Appendix IV

Acts 6 v 1 – 7 v 60 (Read in conjunction with Chapter 40)

Acts Chapter 6

1 And in those days, when the number of the disciples was multiplied, there arose a murmuring of the Grecians against the Hebrews, because their widows were neglected in the daily ministration.

2 Then the twelve called the multitude of the disciples unto them, and said, It is not reason that we should leave the word of God, and serve tables.

3 Wherefore, brethren, look ye out among you seven men of honest report, full of the Holy Ghost and wisdom, whom we may appoint over this business.

4 But we will give ourselves continually to prayer, and to the ministry of the word.

5 And the saying pleased the whole multitude: and they chose Stephen, a man full of faith and of the Holy Ghost, and Philip, and Prochorus, and Nicanor, and Timon, and Parmenas, and Nicolas a proselyte of Antioch:

6 Whom they set before the apostles: and when they had prayed, they laid their hands on them.

7 And the word of God increased; and the number of the disciples multiplied in Jerusalem greatly; and a great company of the priests were obedient to the faith.

8 And Stephen, full of faith and power, did great wonders and miracles among the people.

9 Then there arose certain of the synagogue, which is called the synagogue of the Libertines, and Cyrenians, and Alexandrians, and of them of Cilicia and of Asia, disputing with Stephen.

10 And they were not able to resist the wisdom and the spirit by which he spake.

11 Then they suborned men, which said, We have heard him speak blasphemous words against Moses, and against God.

12 And they stirred up the people, and the elders, and the scribes, and

came upon him, and caught him, and brought him to the council,

13 And set up false witnesses, which said, This man ceaseth not to speak blasphemous words against this holy place, and the law:

14 For we have heard him say, that this Jesus of Nazareth shall destroy this place, and shall change the customs which Moses delivered us.

15 And all that sat in the council, looking steadfastly on him, saw his face as it had been the face of an angel.

Acts Chapter 7

1 Then said the high priest, Are these things so?

2 And he said, Men, brethren, and fathers, hearken: The God of glory appeared unto our father Abraham, when he was in Mesopotamia, before he dwelt in Haran,

3 And said unto him, Get thee out of thy country, and from thy kindred, and come into the land which I shall show thee.

4 Then came he out of the land of the Chaldeans, and dwelt in Haran; and from there, when his father was dead, he removed him into this land, in which ye now dwell.

5 And he gave him no inheritance in it, no, not so much as to set his foot on; yet he promised that he would give it to him for a possession, and to his seed after him, when as yet he had no child.

6 And God spoke in this way, That his seed should sojourn in a strange land; and that they should bring them into bondage, and ii-treat them evil four hundred years.

7 And the nation to whom they shall be in bondage will I judge, said God; and after that shall they come forth, and serve me in this place.

8 And he gave him the covenant of circumcision; and so Abraham begot Isaac, and circumcised him the eighth day; and Isaac begot Jacob; and Jacob begot the twelve patriarchs.

9 And the patriarchs, moved with envy, sold Joseph into Egypt; but God was with him,

10 And delivered him out of all his afflictions, and gave him favour and wisdom in the sight of Pharaoh, king of Egypt; and he made him governor over Egypt and all his house.

11 Now there came a famine over all the land of Egypt and Canaan,

and great affliction; and our fathers found no sustenance.

12 But when Jacob heard that there was grain in Egypt, he sent out our fathers first.

13 And at the second time Joseph was made known to his brethren; and Joseph's kindred was made known unto Pharaoh.

14 Then sent Joseph, and called his father Jacob to him, and all his kindred, threescore and fifteen souls.

15 So Jacob went down into Egypt, and died, he, and our fathers,

16 And were carried over into Shechem, and laid in the sepulchre that Abraham bought for a sum of money of the sons of Hamor the father of Shechem.

17 But when the time of the promise drew near, which God had sworn to Abraham, the people grew and multiplied in Egypt,

18 Till another king arose, which knew not Joseph.

19 The same dealt craftily with our kindred, and ill-treated our fathers, so that they cast out their young children, to the end they might not live.

20 In which time Moses was born, and was exceeding fair, and nourished up in his father's house three months;

21 And when he was cast out, Pharaoh's daughter took him up, and nourished him for her own son.

22 And Moses was learned in all the wisdom of the Egyptians, and was mighty in words and in deeds.

23 And when he was full forty years old, it came into his heart to visit his brethren. the children of Israel.

24 And seeing one of them suffer wrong, he defended him, and avenged him that was oppressed, and smote the Egyptian.

25 For he supposed his brethren would have understood how that God by his hand would deliver them; but they understood not.

26 And the next day he showed himself unto them as they strove, and would have set them at one again, saying, Sirs, ye are brethren; why do ye wrong one to another?

27 But he that did his neighbour wrong thrust him away, saying, Who made thee a ruler and a judge over us?

28 Wilt thou kill me, as thou diddest the Egyptian yesterday?

29 Then fled Moses at this saying, and was a sojourner in the land of Median, where he begot two sons.

30 And when forty years were expired, there appeared to him in the wilderness of mount Sinai an angel of the Lord in a flame of fire in a bush.

31 When Moses saw it, he wondered at the sight; and as he drew near to behold it, the voice of the Lord came unto him,

32 Saying, I am the God of thy fathers, the God of Abraham, and the God of Isaac, and the God of Jacob. Then Moses trembled, and dare not behold.

33 Then said the Lord to him, Put off thy shoes from thy feet; for the place where thou standest is holy ground.

34 I have seen, I have seen the affliction of my people which is in Egypt, and I have heard their groaning, and am come down to deliver them. And now come, I will send thee into Egypt.

35 This Moses whom they refused, saying, Who made thee a ruler and a judge? the same did God send to be a ruler and a deliverer by the hand of the angel who appeared to him in the bush.

36 He brought them out, after that he had shown wonders and signs in the land of Egypt, and in the Red sea, and in the wilderness forty years.

37 This is that Moses who said unto the children of Israel, A prophet shall the Lord, your God, raise up unto you of your brethren, like unto me; him shall ye hear.

38 This is he that was in the church in the wilderness with the angel who spake to him in Mount Sinai, and with our fathers, who received the living oracles to give unto us;

39 Whom our fathers would not obey, but thrust him from them, and in their hearts turned back again into Egypt,

40 Saying unto Aaron, Make us gods to go before us; for, as for this Moses who brought us out of the land of Egypt, we know not what is become of him.

41 And they made a calf in those days, and offered sacrifice unto the idol, and rejoiced in the works of their own hands.

42 Then God turned, and gave them up to worship the host of heaven; as it is written in the book of the prophets, O ye house of Israel, have ye offered to me slain beasts and sacrifices by the space of forty years in the wilderness?

43 Yea, ye took up the tabernacle of Molech, and the star of your god Rephan, figures which ye made to worship; and I will carry you

away beyond Babylon.

44 Our fathers had the tabernacle of witness in the wilderness, as he had appointed, speaking unto Moses, that he should make it according to the fashion that he had seen;

45 Which also our fathers that came after brought in with Joshua into the possession of the nations, whom God drove out before the face of our fathers, unto the days of David,

46 Who found favour before God, and desired to find a tabernacle for the God of Jacob.

47 But Solomon built him an house.

48 Nevertheless, the Most High dwelleth not in temples made with hands, as saith the prophet,

49 Heaven is my throne, and earth is my footstool. What house will ye build me? saith the Lord. Or what is the place of my rest?

50 Hath not my hand made all these things?

51 Ye stiff-necked and uncircumcised in heart and ears, ye do always resist the Holy Spirit; as your fathers did, so do ye.

52 Which of the prophets have not your fathers persecuted? and they have slain them who showed before of the coming of the Just One, of whom ye have been now the betrayers and murderers;

53 Who have received the law by the disposition of angels, and have not kept it.

54 When they heard these things, they were cut to the heart, and they gnashed on him with their teeth.

55 But he, being full of the Holy Ghost, looked up steadfastly into heaven, and saw the glory of God, and Jesus standing on the right hand of God,

56 And said, Behold, I see the heavens opened, and the Son of man standing on the right hand of God.

57 Then they cried out with a loud voice, and stopped their ears, and ran upon him with one accord,

58 And cast him out of the city, and stoned him; and the witnesses laid down their clothes at a young man's feet, whose name was Saul.

59 And they stoned Stephen, calling upon God, and saying, Lord Jesus, receive my spirit.

60 And he kneeled down, and cried with a loud voice, Lord, lay not this sin to their charge. And when he had said this, he fell asleep.

Appendix V

List of Everyday Sayings covered in the first book
(Everyday Sayings & The Bible)

A bow at a venture
A Damascus Road experience
A Judas / A Judas Iscariot / A Judas kiss
A law unto oneself!
A little bird told me!
A man after my own heart!
A matter of life and death
A thorn in the side
A wolf in sheep's clothing
Acted the fool
An eye for an eye and a tooth for a tooth
An olive branch
Between a rock and a hard place
By the skin of one's teeth
Doesn't suffer fools gladly
Go from strength to strength
Go on all fours
God forbid!
He couldn't tie his laces!
Head and shoulders above the rest
Hold your whist!
It's a godsend
Job's comforters
Keep your mouth shut
Kept the good wine until the last
Learnt from/by experience
Less or more!
Made a scapegoat
Make hay while the sun shines
Manna from heaven
Many are called but few are chosen

Money is the root of all evil
My hair stood on end! On your head be it!!
Practice what you preach!
Putting out the fleece
Root and branch
Safe and sound
So far and no farther!
Spit in one's face!
Taking your life in your own hands!
The blind leading the blind!
The Jews have no dealings with the Samaritans
The patience of Job!
The root of the matter
The salt of the earth!
The tail wagging the dog
The writing's on the wall
Will not lift a finger to help
You haven't heard the half of it!